QI Macros Example Book

Jay Arthur

QI Macros Example Book
© 2010 by Jay Arthur

Published by KnowWare International
2253 S. Oneida St. Ste 3D
Denver, CO 80224-2518
(888) 468-1537 or (303) 756-9144 (phone)
(888) 468-1536 or (303) 753-3107 (fax)
info@qimacros.com
www.qimacros.com

Upgrade Your KnowWare®!

Also by Jay Arthur:
Lean Six Sigma DeMYSTiFieD, A Self Teaching Guide, McGraw Hill, 2006
Six Sigma Simplified (3rd), Breakthrough Improvement Made Easy, LifeStar, 2004
The Six Sigma Instructor's Guide (2nd), Greenbelt Training Made Easy, LifeStar, 2003

Phone, Fax, or E-mail support: Contact KnowWare International Inc at the phone, fax or e-mail address above for any questions you have about Six Sigma or using this book.

On-site Workshops:

- **QI Macros and Data Mining One Day:** qimacros.com/qimacros-training.html
- **Lean Six Sigma Simplified One-Day:** qimacros.com/lean-six-sigma-workshop.html
- **Lean for Healthcare Labs Two-Days:** qimacros.com/lean-lab-workshop.html

Free downloads available from www.qimacros.com/freestuff.html

- QI Macros SPC Software for Excel 30-day Trial copy
- QI Macros User Guide (1Mb PDF)
- Free Lean and Six Sigma Ebooks, Action Plan and Quick Reference Cards

Other Free Resources on www.qimacros.com:

- QI Macros and Lean Six Sigma Webinars: check available dates and register at: qimacros.com/webinars/webinar-dates.html
- QI Macros Video Tour at qimacros.com/qimacros-video-tour.htm
- QI Macros lessons and articles at qimacros.com/qimacros-excel-tips.html
- QI Macros formulas at qimacros.com/formulas.html
- QI Macros FAQs at qimacros.com/macrofaqs.html

Six Sigma is a registered trade and service mark of Motorola, Inc.

Table of Contents

Six Sigma Simplified
Laser-Focused Improvement

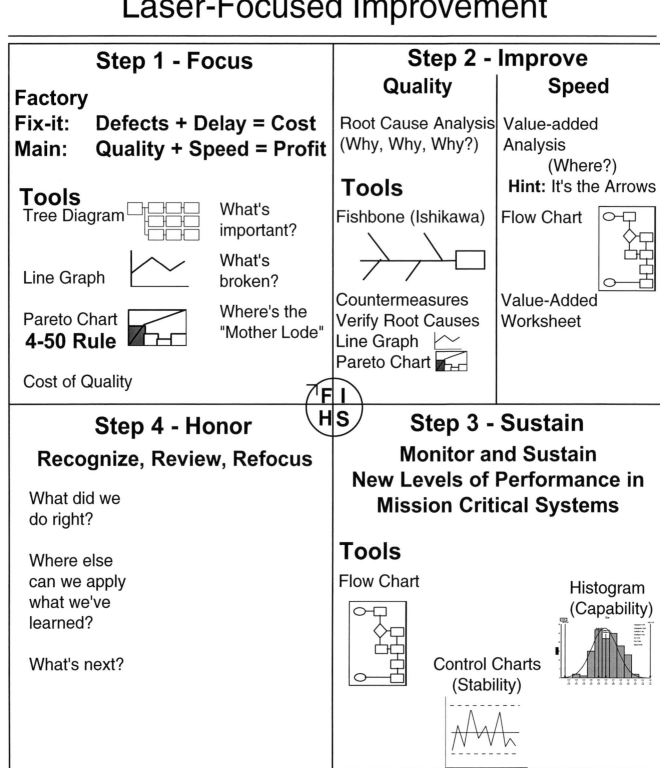

Step 1 - Focus

Factory
Fix-it: **Defects + Delay = Cost**
Main: **Quality + Speed = Profit**

Tools

Tree Diagram — What's important?

Line Graph — What's broken?

Pareto Chart
4-50 Rule — Where's the "Mother Lode"

Cost of Quality

Step 2 - Improve

Quality

Root Cause Analysis (Why, Why, Why?)

Tools

Fishbone (Ishikawa)

Countermeasures
Verify Root Causes
Line Graph
Pareto Chart

Speed

Value-added Analysis (Where?)
Hint: It's the Arrows

Flow Chart

Value-Added Worksheet

F I H S

Step 4 - Honor

Recognize, Review, Refocus

What did we do right?

Where else can we apply what we've learned?

What's next?

Step 3 - Sustain

Monitor and Sustain
New Levels of Performance in
Mission Critical Systems

Tools

Flow Chart

Histogram (Capability)

Control Charts (Stability)

Attribute	Variable
np, p	XmR
c,u	XbarR
	XbarS

Using the QI Macros Overview
Prepare Your Data

Why?

When?

Before drawing your charts.

How?

Here's how easy it is to create a chart using the QI Macros:

1. Select the labels and data.
2. Run any chart
3. See what you can learn from the chart (e.g., Is the process stable or capable? Is there a problem you can solve?)

When your data is set up properly, it will be much easier to draw the graphs and interpret the results.

1. Worksheet Format: Other software packages make you transfer your Excel data into special tables, but not the QI Macros. Just put your data in a standard Excel worksheet. The simplest format for your data is usually one column of labels, and one or more columns of data (e.g., samples):

	A	B	C	D	E	F
	Sample	1	2	3	4	5
	6/8 8am	0.65	0.7	0.65	0.65	0.85
	10am	0.75	0.85	0.75	0.85	0.65
	12pm	0.75	0.8	0.8	0.7	0.75
	2pm	0.6	0.7	0.7	0.75	0.65
	6/9 8am	0.7	0.75	0.65	0.85	0.8
	10am	0.6	0.75	0.75	0.85	0.7
	12pm	0.75	0.8	0.65	0.75	0.7
	2pm	0.6	0.7	0.8	0.75	0.75

Your data can also be in horizontal format (one row of headers, and one or more rows of data).

Required number of columns of data:			
1	1 or more	2	2 or more
Pareto	Line, Bar	Scatter	Box & Whisker
Pie, Run	Histogram		Multivari
c, np, XmR	Freq Hist	u Chart	XbarR
Levey Jennings	EWMA	p Chart	XandS
Moving Avg	Cusum	Hotelling	Matrix Plot
Dot Plot	Xmedian R		

2. **Selecting Your Data:** Then, just use your mouse to click-and-drag to select the data you want to graph. (Hint: don't select the whole column, just the rows you want to graph.)

3. Select desired chart from the QI Macros pull-down menu.

QI Macros Example Book

Using the QI Macros Overview
Summarize Your Data (Optional)

Excel's Pivot Table Wizard will summarize your data just about any way you want.

1. Select the labels and data to be summarized, in this case individual event codes by region.

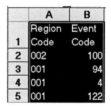

	A	B
	Region Code	Event Code
1		
2	002	100
3	001	94
4	001	4
5	001	122

2. From Excel's pull-down menu, choose: Data - Pivot Table.
Follow the Pivot-Table Wizard until you get a screen like one of these:

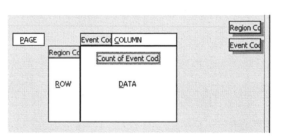

3. Click and drag the data labels into the appropriate area of the pivot table to get the summarization you want:

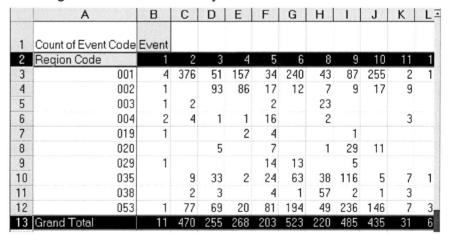

	A	B	C	D	E	F	G	H	I	J	K	L
1	Count of Event Code	Event										
2	Region Code	1	2	3	4	5	6	8	9	10	11	1
3	001	4	376	51	157	34	240	43	87	255	2	1
4	002	1		93	86	17	12	7	9	17	9	
5	003	1	2			2		23				
6	004	2	4	1	1	16		2			3	
7	019	1			2	4			1			
8	020			5		7		1	29	11		
9	029	1				14	13		5			
10	035		9	33	2	24	63	38	116	5	7	1
11	038		2	3		4	1	57	2	1	3	
12	053	1	77	69	20	81	194	49	236	146	7	3
13	Grand Total	11	470	255	268	203	523	220	485	435	31	6

4. Select labels and totals, and draw pareto and other charts using your summarized data.

Note: The QI Macros Pivot Table Wizard makes Pivot Tables easy. Select up to 4 four columns of data and select Data Transformation Tools and then: Pivot Table Wizard - CrossTab. The QI Macros will analyze your data and create a Pivot Table for you.

Column/Bar Chart

Why?
Highlights differences between groups or categories

When?
Comparing discrete results.

How?
1. Run the Column or Bar Chart
2. Look for obvious differences (e.g., Plant 2's defects are declining while others vary).

Data
defects by plant

	A	B	C	D
1		Plant 1	Plant 2	Plant 3
2	Jan	15	77	44
3	Feb	23	56	33
4	Mar	56	33	55
5	Apr	33	33	22
6	May	77	23	66
7	Jun	33	15	11
8	Jul	14	14	77

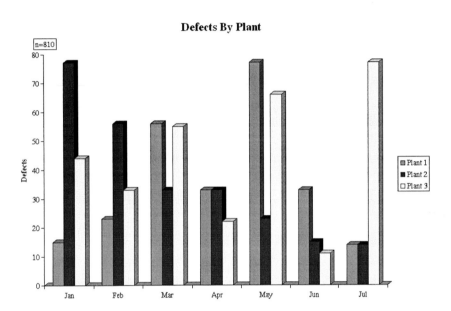

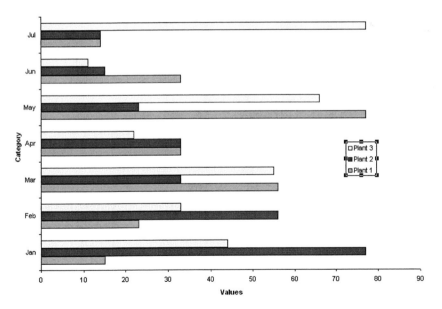

What can you learn?
Plant 1: Varies month to month with a spike in May (special cause?)

Plant 2: Decreasing defects each month (What are they doing to reduce defects? How can we share what they're learning with the other plants?)

Plant 3: Alternately increasing and decreasing every other month. (Overreacting each month to the previous month?)

Radar or Spider Chart

Why?

When?

Comparing discrete results.

How?

1. Run the Radar/ Spider Chart
2. Each of the spokes represents one observation of one or more (multi-variate) data points (in this case defects for three different plants).
3. Look for obvious differences (e.g., Plant 2's defects are declining while others vary).

Data

defects by plant

	A	B	C	D
1		Plant 1	Plant 2	Plant 3
2	Jan	15	77	44
3	Feb	23	56	33
4	Mar	56	33	55
5	Apr	33	33	22
6	May	77	23	66
7	Jun	33	15	11
8	Jul	14	14	77

Highlights differences in multivariate data (e.g., defects by plant):

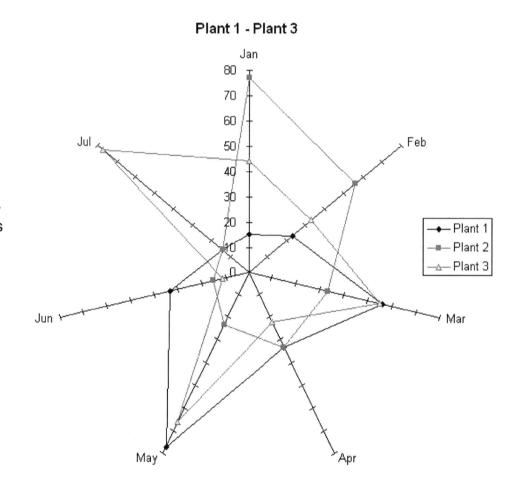

Plant 1 - Plant 3

What can you learn?

Plant 1: Varies month to month with a spike in May (outlier?).

Plant 2: Decreasing defects each month. (What are they doing to reduce defects? How can we share what they're learning with the other plants?)

Plant 3: Alternately increasing and decreasing every other month. (Overreacting each month to the previous month?)

Box and Whisker Chart

Why?

When?

Monitor process with two or more samples of variable data per period or device.

How?

1. Select the labels, and 2 or more samples.
2. Run the Box & Whisker Chart
3. Analyze the chart for obvious variation or trends.

Data

Diameters (5 samples)

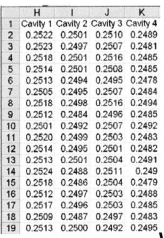

	A	B	C	D	E	F
Sample	1	2	3	4	5	
6/8 8am	0.65	0.7	0.65	0.65	0.85	
10am	0.75	0.85	0.75	0.85	0.65	
12pm	0.75	0.8	0.8	0.7	0.75	
2pm	0.6	0.7	0.7	0.75	0.65	
6/9 8am	0.7	0.75	0.65	0.85	0.8	
10am		0.6	0.75	0.75	0.85	0.7
12pm	0.75		0.8	0.65	0.75	0.7
2pm		0.6	0.7		0.8	0.75	0.75

Cavities (4 different)

	H	I	J	K
1	Cavity 1	Cavity 2	Cavity 3	Cavity 4
2	0.2522	0.2501	0.2510	0.2489
3	0.2523	0.2497	0.2507	0.2481
4	0.2518	0.2501	0.2516	0.2485
5	0.2514	0.2501	0.2508	0.2485
6	0.2513	0.2494	0.2495	0.2478
7	0.2505	0.2495	0.2507	0.2484
8	0.2518	0.2498	0.2516	0.2494
9	0.2512	0.2484	0.2496	0.2485
10	0.2501	0.2492	0.2507	0.2492
11	0.2520	0.2499	0.2503	0.2483
12	0.2514	0.2495	0.2501	0.2482
13	0.2513	0.2501	0.2504	0.2491
14	0.2524	0.2488	0.2511	0.249
15	0.2518	0.2486	0.2504	0.2479
16	0.2512	0.2497	0.2503	0.2488
17	0.2517	0.2496	0.2503	0.2485
18	0.2509	0.2487	0.2497	0.2483
19	0.2513	0.2500	0.2492	0.2495

To analyze variation and central tendency of the data due to time, parts, and production tools. Box shows 2nd and 3rd quartiles of the data (center). Whisker shows up to 1.5 times the box. "x" designates points outside the whisker.

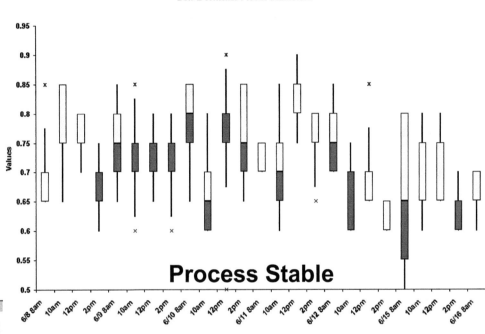

Box & Whisker Plot of Diameters

Process Stable

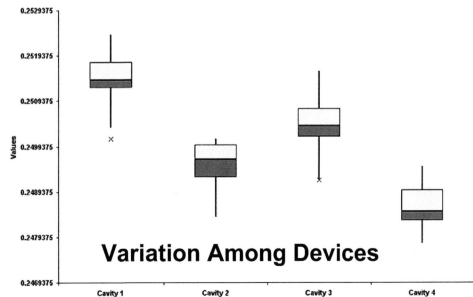

Cavity Measurement

Variation Among Devices

What can you learn? Processes for drilling cavities is stable (same size box & whisker), but off-target.

Frequency Histogram

Why?

When?

Analyze distribution of data.

How?

1. Run the Frequency Histogram
2. Evaluate central tendency (Cpk), distribution, and capability (Cp) of your process.

Data

Diameters

A	B	C	D	E	F
Sample	1	2	3	4	5
6/8 8am	0.65	0.7	0.65	0.65	0.85
10am	0.75	0.85	0.75	0.85	0.65
12pm	0.75	0.8	0.8	0.7	0.75
2pm	0.6	0.7	0.7	0.75	0.65
6/9 8am	0.7	0.75	0.65	0.85	0.8
10am	0.6	0.75	0.75	0.85	0.7
12pm	0.75	0.8	0.65	0.75	0.7
2pm	0.6	0.7	0.8	0.75	0.75

Cp, Cpk

Sigma	Cp/Cpk
3	1.0
4	1.33
5	1.67
6	2.0

Evaluate the *distribution* of your data and capability of your process when the variable data falls into predictable sizes (e.g., 0.65, 0.70, 0.75)

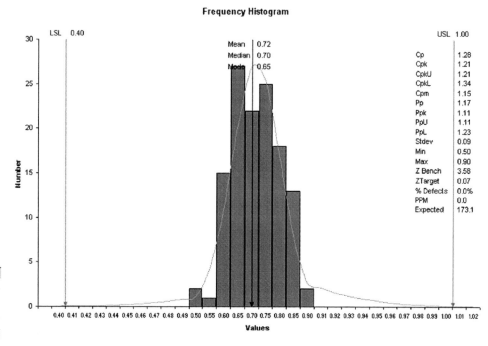

What can you learn?

Cp > 1 - Process is capable (products fall between upper and lower specification limits), and between 3-4 Sigma (Cp=1.0-to-1.33). Process could be improved by reducing variation and tightening up the production around a target (e.g., 0.7).

Cpk > 1 - Process is capable and centered. Because Cp = Cpk (approximately), process is *centered* between LSL and USL, not shifted either direction. (Don't need to shift the process mean, just reduce variation.)

Normal - If you look at the chart you can see that the bars are closely aligned to the normal curve: you have a *normal* distribution.

Use Cp, Cpk when you have a sample. Cp, Cpk use sigma estimator. Use Pp, Ppk when you have the total population. Pp, Ppk use standard deviation. If Cp, Pp are fairly different, then you may have an unstable process. Run a control chart on your data to analyze stability.

Histogram

Why?

When?

Analyze capability of the process.

How?

1. Run the Histogram
3. Evaluate central tendency, distribution, and capability of your process.

Data

Diameters

A	B	C	D	E	F
	Obs 1	Obs 2	Obs 3	Obs 4	Obs 5
S1	74.030	74.002	74.019	73.992	74.008
S2	73.995	73.992	74.001	74.011	74.004
S3	73.988	74.024	74.021	74.005	74.002
S4	74.002	73.996	73.993	74.015	74.009
S5	73.992	74.007	74.015	73.989	74.014
S6	74.009	73.994	73.997	73.985	73.993
S7	73.995	74.006	73.994	74.000	74.005
S8	73.985	74.003	73.993	74.015	73.988
S9	74.008	73.995	74.009	74.005	74.004
S10	73.998	74.000	73.990	74.007	73.995

Cp, Cpk

Sigma	Cp/Cpk
3	1.0
4	1.33
5	1.67
6	2.0

Evaluate the <u>capability</u> of a process to meet customer's specifications using **measured** (i.e., variable) data like time, money, age, length, width, and weight.

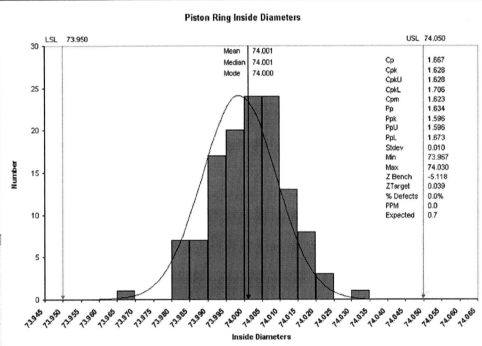

Mean	74.001		Cp	1.667
Median	74.001		Cpk	1.628
Mode	74.000		CpkU	1.628
			CpkL	1.706
			Cpm	1.623
			Pp	1.634
			Ppk	1.596
			PpU	1.596
			PpL	1.673
			Stdev	0.010
			Min	73.967
			Max	74.030
			Z Bench	-5.118
			ZTarget	0.039
			% Defects	0.0%
			PPM	0.0
			Expected	0.7

LSL 73.950   USL 74.050

Piston Ring Inside Diameters

What can you learn?

Cp > 1 - Process is capable (products fall between upper and lower specification limits), and between 3-4 Sigma (Cp=1.0-to-1.33). Process could be improved by reducing variation and tightening up the production around a target (e.g., 74.0).

Cpk > 1 - Process is capable and centered. Because Cp = Cpk, process is *centered* between LSL and USL, not shifted either direction. (Don't need to shift the process mean, just reduce variation.)

Normal - If you look at the chart you can see that the bars are closely aligned to the normal curve: you have a *normal* distribution.

Use Cp, Cpk when you have a sample. Cp, Cpk use sigma estimator. Use Pp, Ppk when you have the total population. Pp, Ppk use standard deviation. If Cp, Pp are fairly different, then you may have an unstable process. Run a control chart on your data to analyze stability.

Line Graph

Why?
When?

Measure and monitor processes over time. This is the first step of the improvement process-defining a problem to be solved.

How?

1. Select the labels and data.
2. Run the Line graph.
3. Evaluate trends. (You cannot determine much about process performance and stability from a line graph alone.)
4. Rerun using control chart to evaluate stability.

Data

Defects by Month

	A	B
1		Plant 1
2	Jan	15
3	Feb	23
4	Mar	56
5	Apr	33
6	May	77
7	Jun	33
8	Jul	14

Measure and analyze process performance *over time*.
There are two ways of looking at problems:

Increase (want more of a "good" thing)
Decrease (want less of a "bad" thing, e.g., defects)

These are often two sides of the same coin:

an increase in ...	is equal to a decrease in . . .
quality	number or percent defective
speed	cycle time–to deliver a product or service
	idle time–people, materials, machines
profitability	cost of waste and rework

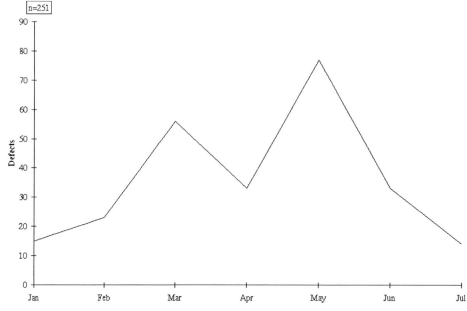

Defects by Month - Plant 1

What can you learn?

Line graphs give you a quick impression of performance, but they don't give you insight into the average (run chart) or whether the process is stable and predictable (control charts). So consider using one of the control charts to maximize your understanding of the process and its performance.

Matrix Plot

Why?

When?

Evaluate cause-effect relationships in more than two variables.

How?

1. Select the labels and two columns of data.
2. Run the Matrix Plot.
3. Look for tight, linear relationships.

Data

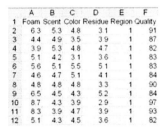

	A	B	C	D	E	F
1	Foam	Scent	Color	Residue	Region	Quality
2	6.3	5.3	4.8	3.1	1	91
3	4.4	4.9	3.5	3.9	1	87
4	3.9	5.3	4.8	4.7	1	82
5	5.1	4.2	3.1	3.6	1	83
6	5.6	5.1	5.5	5.1	1	83
7	4.6	4.7	5.1	4.1	1	84
8	4.8	4.8	4.8	3.3	1	90
9	6.5	4.5	4.3	5.2	1	84
10	8.7	4.3	3.9	2.9	1	97
11	8.3	3.9	4.7	3.9	1	93
12	5.1	4.3	4.5	3.6	1	82

Evaluate correlations and cause-effects between two or more variables. It's a great way to take a quick look at many interactions.

In this case, we're evaluating shampoo for the relationships between Foam, Scent, Color, Residue, Region, Quality.

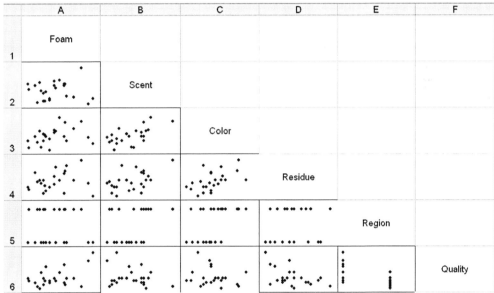

It looks like there might be a cause-effect relationship between:
- **scent and color (B3)**
- **color and residue (C4)**
- **everything else looks like a shotgun blast**

Also, Region 1 (E6) has higher quality ratings than Region 2.

Multivari Chart

Why?

When?

Monitor process with two or more samples of variable data per period.

How?

1. Select the labels and 2 or more samples.
2. Run the Multivari chart. (Also consider using the Box & Whisker Chart.)
3. Analyze the chart for obvious variation or trends.

Data

	A	B	C	D
	Size of		Customer	Overall
1	Customer	Product Type	Type	Satisfaction
2	Small	Consumer	2	3.54
3	Large	Consumer	3	3.16
4	Small	Manufacturer	2	2.42
5	Large	Manufacturer	2	2.7
6	Small	Consumer	3	3.31
7	Large	Consumer	2	4.12
8	Large	Manufacturer	1	3.24
9	Large	Manufacturer	2	4.47
10	Large	Consumer	2	3.83
11	Small	Consumer	1	2.94

Evaluate process variability due to differences between categories.

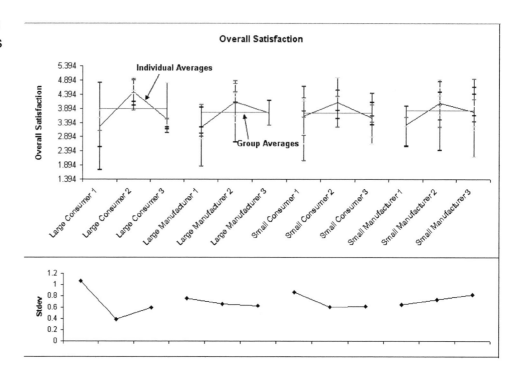

What can you learn?

The Multivari chart shows the high and low values as well as each point in the sample. The spread gives you some idea of the variation. It also shows the individual and group averages.

The Multivari chart also creates a standard deviation plot for each group as well.

Pareto Chart

Why?

When?

To laser-focus improvement efforts on the 4% of your business that creates over 50% of the waste, rework, and cost.

How?

1. Select the labels and one or more columns of data.
2. Run the Pareto Chart
3. Look for 1-3 "big bars" and many smaller ones.
4. If you have more detail for each of the "big bars", run additional Pareto charts for lower level data.
5. Create an Ishikawa diagram for each "big bar."

Data

	D	E	F	G
15		Staffing by Shift		
16		7-3	3-11	11-7
17	Under	13	28	2
18	Over	1	2	4

Analyze and prioritize key contributors to a problem to allow you to laser-focus your improvement efforts.

Begin by identifying the <u>components</u> of the problem:

Indicator	Pareto Components
Defects	- types of defects
Time	- steps or delays in a process
Cost	- types of costs–rework, waste

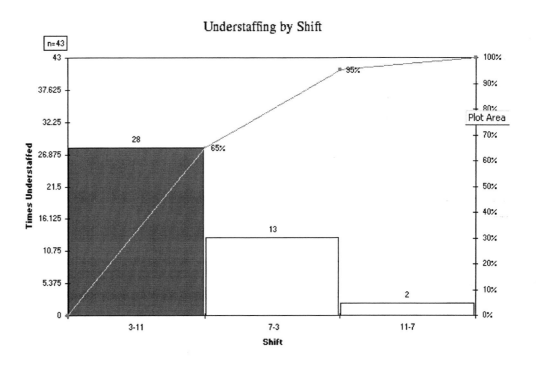

Understaffing by Shift

What can you learn?

The 3-11 shift is understaffed 65% of the time, which is over twice as high as the 7-3 shift. So the 3-11 shift would be the key one to focus on to reduce understaffing.

Pie Chart

Why?

Show how various parts relate to the whole.

When?

Show relative size of contribution of various components of defects, time or cost.

How?

1. Select the labels and data.
2. Run the Pie Chart
3. Evaluate vital few contributors.

Data

Defects/Month

	A	B
1		Plant 1
2	Jan	15
3	Feb	23
4	Mar	56
5	Apr	33
6	May	77
7	Jun	33
8	Jul	14

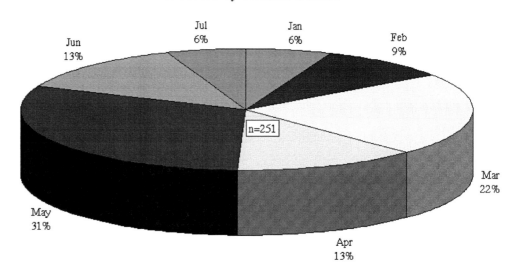

Defects by Month Plant1

What can you learn?

The pie chart is like the Pareto, but it doesn't show you the biggest contributor first (May at 31%) unless you sort your data.

Run Chart

Why?   Measure and analyze process performance *over time*.

When?

Measure and monitor processes over time. This is the first step of the improvement process-defining a problem to be solved.

How?

1. Select the labels and data.
2. Run the Run chart.
3. Evaluate trends. (You cannot determine a lot about process performance and stability from a run chart alone.)
4. Rerun using control chart to evaluate stability.

Data

Hours Missed

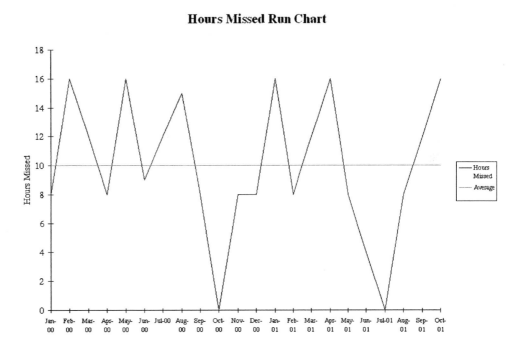

Hours Missed Run Chart

What can you learn?

The Run chart is just a line graph with another line added to show the average of the data. These can give you a quick read on what you can expect from your process. It won't, however, tell you if the process is stable. You'll need a control chart to tell you about stability.

One thing you might add to this chart is a target line or specification limits. You can do this using Excel's drawing toolbar (View-Toolbars-Drawing). Just draw lines right on the chart.

	A	B
1		Hours Missed
2	Jan-00	8
3	Feb-00	16
4	Mar-00	12
5	Apr-00	8
6	May-00	16
7	Jun-00	9
8	Jul-00	12

Scatter Chart

Why?

Evaluate correlations and cause-effects between two variables.

When?

Evaluate cause-effect relationships (e.g., after root cause analysis.)

How?

1. Select the labels and two columns of data.
2. Run the Scatter Chart
3. Evaluate the "linearity" or "scatter" of the data. If it looks like shotgun pellets, there's no correlation. R^2 close to 1.0 means a perfect fit.

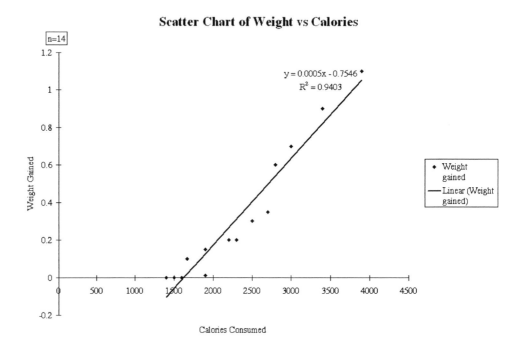

Scatter Chart of Weight vs Calories

$y = 0.0005x - 0.7546$
$R^2 = 0.9403$

n=14

Data

	B	C
17	Calories Consumed	Weight gained
18	1500	0
19	2300	0.2
20	3400	0.9
21	2200	0.2
22	2500	0.3
23	1600	0
24	1400	0
25	1900	0.01
26	2800	0.6
27	3900	1.1
28	1670	0.1
29	1900	0.15
30	2700	0.35
31	3000	0.7

What can you learn?

When you think there's a cause-effect link between two indicators (e.g., calories consumed and weight gain) then you can use the scatter diagram to prove or disprove it. If the points are tightly clustered along the trend line, then there's probably a strong correlation. If it looks more like a shotgun blast, there is no correlation.

If the R^2 (correlation of determination shown on the data sheet, which is the square of the correlation coefficient) is greater than 0.8, then 80% of the variability in the data is accounted for by the equation. Most statistics books imply that this means that you have a strong correlation.

Understanding Standard Deviation and Control Charts

Many people ask: "Why aren't my upper and lower control limits (UCL, LCL) calculated as: $\mu \pm 3^*\sigma$ (where μ is the mean and σ is the standard deviation)?"

To answer this question, you have to understand some key principles and underlying statistics: variation, standard deviation, sampling and populations.

Variance

Variance (σ^2) is the average of the square of the distance between each point in a total population (N) and the mean (μ).

$$\sigma^2 = \frac{\sum_{i=1}^{N}(x_i - \mu)^2}{N}$$

Same Mean

Different Standard Deviations

If your data is spread over a wider range, you have a higher variance and standard deviation. If the data is centered around the average, you have a smaller variance and standard deviation.

Standard deviation (σ) is the square root of the variance (σ^2):

Standard Deviation

$$\sigma = \sqrt{\sigma^2}$$

And it can be *estimated* using the average range (R) or stdev(s):

$$\hat{\sigma} = \frac{\bar{R}}{d_2} \qquad \hat{\sigma} = \frac{\bar{s}}{c_4}$$

Sampling

Sampling: Early users of SPC found that it cost too much to evaluate every item in the total population. To reduce the cost of measuring everything, they had to find a way to evaluate a **small sample** and make inferences from it about the **total population**.

Understanding Standard Deviation and Control Charts

Understanding Control Chart Limits: Ask yourself this question: "If a simple formula using the mean and standard deviation would work, *why are there so many different control charts?*" Short answer: to save money by measuring small samples, not the entire population.

When using small samples or varying populations the simple formula using the mean and standard deviation just doesn't work, because **you don't know the μ or σ of the *total population*, only your sample**. So why are there so many control charts? Because:

Estimated μ and σ

You have to *estimate* μ and σ using the average and range of your samples. The formulas to do this vary depending on the type of data (variable or attribute) and the sample size. Each control chart's formulas are designed for these varying conditions.

In variable charts, the XmR uses a sample size of 1, XbarR (2-10) and XbarS (11-25). These small samples may be taken from lots of 1,000 or more. In attribute charts, the c and np chart use small samples and "fixed" populations; the u and p charts use varying populations. So, you have to adjust the formulas to compensate for the varying samples and populations.

To reduce the cost of inspection at Western Electric in the 1930s, Dr. Walter S. Shewhart developed a set of formulas and constants to compensate for these variations in sample size and population. That's why they are sometimes called Shewhart Control Charts. You can find these in *any* book on statistical process control (e.g., *Introduction to Statistical Process Control*, Montgomery, Wiley, 2001, pgs 207-265).

So stop worrying about the formulas.
Start monitoring your process using the charts.

Choosing the Right Chart

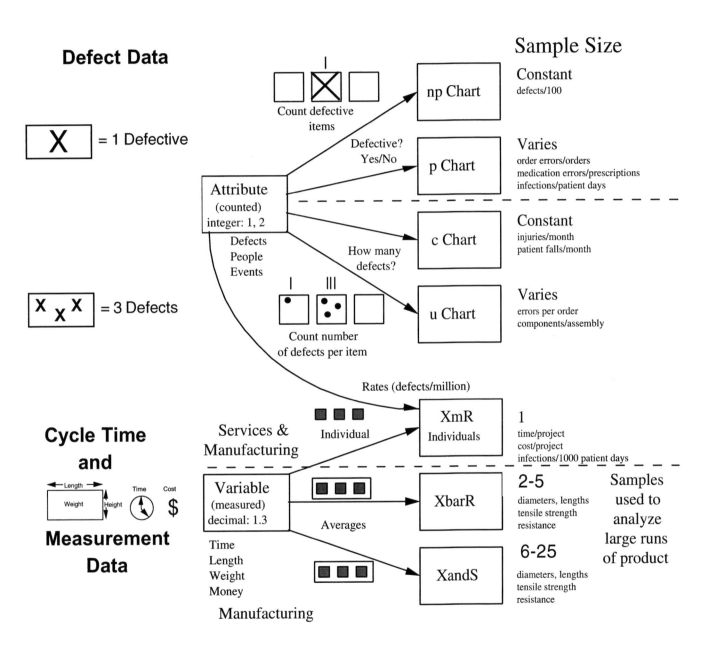

The QI Macros contains a Control Chart Wizard that will analyze your data and select the right control chart for you.

Analyzing Stability

Automation

The QI Macros will identify any of these potentially unstable conditions in red.

Processes that are "out of control" need to be stabilized before they can be improved using the problem-solving process. Special causes require immediate cause-effect analysis to eliminate the variation.

The following diagram will help you evaluate stability in any control chart. Unstable conditions can be any of the following:

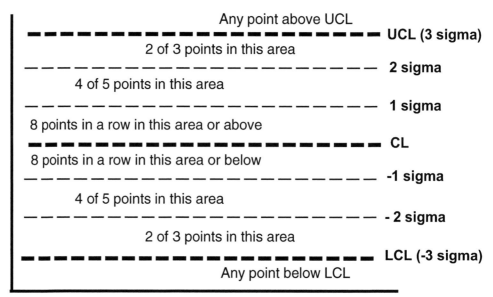

Any of these conditions suggests an unstable condition may exist. Other unstable conditions may be x points in a row increasing or decreasing, alternating up and down or inside or outside of the 1 sigma lines. Consider investigating the special cause of variation.

Use the Ishikawa diagram to analyze potential root causes.

Once you've eliminated the special causes, you can turn your attention to using the problem solving process to reduce the common causes of variation:

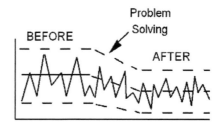

c Chart
Attribute Data (defects), Sample Size Constant

Why?

When?

Monitor process with multiple defects per sample over a given period.

Monitor defects when the opportunity is large compared to the actual number of defects (e.g., patient falls, injuries, etc.) The c chart is useful when it's easy to count the number of defects and the opportunity is large but chance is small (e.g., injuries/month).

How?

1. Select the labels and data.
2. Run the c Chart
3. Evaluate the c chart. Analyze special causes of any instabilities.

Data

Patient Falls

	A	B
1	Month	Total falls
2	Jul-98	17
3	Aug-98	22
4	Sep-98	23
5	Oct-98	30
6	Nov-98	22

	A	B	C
2		No.	Pinholes
3	1	8	
4	2	9	
5	3	5	
6	4	8	
7	5	5	

c Chart Formulas

$$UCL = \bar{c} + 3\sqrt{\bar{c}}$$

$$CL = \bar{c} = \frac{\sum c_i}{n}$$

$$LCL = \bar{c} - 3\sqrt{\bar{c}}$$

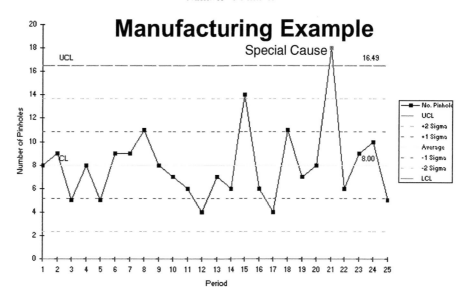

Patient Falls

Service Example

Number of Pinholes

Manufacturing Example

np Chart
Attribute Data (defective), Samples Constant

Why?

When?
Monitor process counting defective samples over a given period.

Monitor and evaluate process stability when counting the fraction defective (i.e., samples are either good or bad) and sample size is constant. Examples include defective parts per 100, restraints with constant number of patients.

How?
1. Select the labels and data.
2. Input the sample size (e.g., 50)
3. Run the np Chart
4. Evaluate the np chart. Analyze special causes of any instabilities.

Data
Defects/ 50 samples

	A	B	C
1		Defects	Sample Size=50
2	a	12	
3	b	15	
4	c	8	
5	d	10	
6	e	4	
7	f	7	

Manufacturing Example

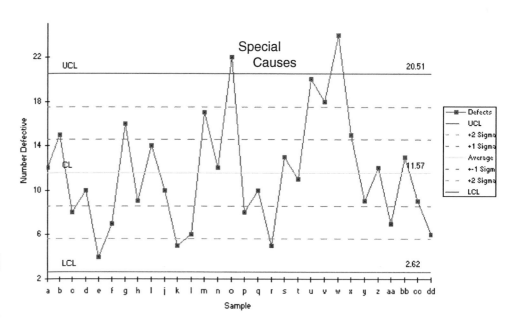

np Chart of Defects

np Chart Formulas

$$UCL = n\bar{p} + 3\sqrt{\left(n\bar{p}(1 - {}^{n\bar{p}}\!/_{n}) \right)}$$

$$CL = n\bar{p} = {\sum np_i}\Big/{n}$$

$$LCL = n\bar{p} - 3\sqrt{\left(n\bar{p}(1 - {}^{n\bar{p}}\!/_{n}) \right)}$$

p Chart
Attribute Data (defective), Sample Size Varies

Why?

When?

Monitor process counting defective samples over a given period.

How?

1. Select the labels and data.
2. Run the p Chart
3. Evaluate the p chart. Analyze special causes of any instabilities.

Data

Patient Falls/Patient Days

	A	B	C
1	Month	Total falls	Total pt days
2	Jul-98	17	4658
3	Aug-98	22	4909
4	Sep-98	23	4886
5	Oct-98	30	4970
6	Nov-98	22	4780

Defects/Samples

	A	B	C
1		Defects	Sample Size
2	Jan-00	21	196
3	Feb-00	25	210
4	Mar-00	28	210
5	Apr-00	27	210
6	May-00	15	210
7	Jun-00	6	174

p Chart Formulas

$$UCL = \bar{p} + 3\sqrt{\left(\frac{\bar{p}(1-\bar{p})}{n_i}\right)}$$

$$CL = \bar{p} = \frac{\sum p_i}{\sum n_i}$$

$$LCL = \bar{p} - 3\sqrt{\left(\frac{\bar{p}(1-\bar{p})}{n_i}\right)}$$

Monitor and evaluate process stability when counting the fraction defective (i.e., samples are either good or bad) when sample size varies. Examples include defective circuit boards, parts, paychecks, or other product or service.

Patient Falls   Patient Days

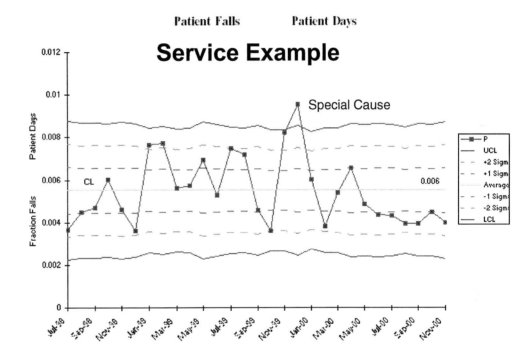

p Chart of Defects

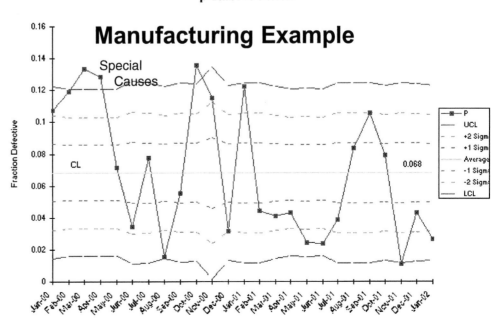

u Chart
Attribute Data (defects), Sample Size Varies

Why?
When?
Monitor process with multiple defects per sample over a given period.

Monitor and evaluate process stability when there can be more than one defect per unit and the sample size varies. Examples might include: the number of defective elements on a circuit board, the number of defects in a dining experience—order wrong, food too cold, check wrong, or the number of defects in a bank statement, invoice, or bill.

How?
1. Select the labels and data.
2. Run the u Chart
3. Evaluate the u chart. Analyze special causes of any instabilities.

Data
Patient Falls/Patient Days

	A	B	C
1	Month	Total falls	Total pt days
2	Jul-98	17	4658
3	Aug-98	22	4909
4	Sep-98	23	4886
5	Oct-98	30	4970
6	Nov-98	22	4780

	A	B	C
1		Defects	Sample Size
2	Jan-00	10	15
3	Feb-00	9	18
4	Mar-00	12	16
5	Apr-00	6	12
6	May-00	15	14
7	Jun-00	3	9

u Chart Formulas

$$UCL = \bar{\bar{u}} + 3\sqrt{\bar{\bar{u}}/n_i}$$

$$CL = \bar{\bar{u}} = \sum u_i / \sum n_i$$

$$u_i = \frac{c_i}{n_i}$$

$$LCL = \bar{\bar{u}} - 3\sqrt{\bar{\bar{u}}/n_i}$$

Patient Falls Per Patient Day

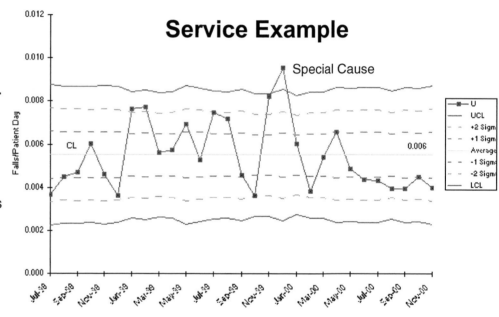

u Chart of Defects

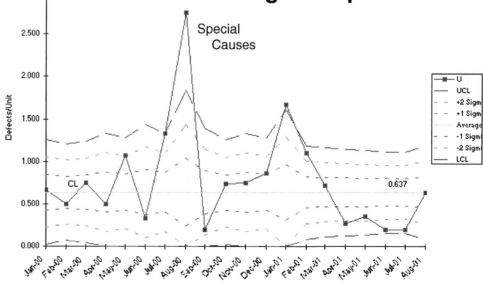

Cusum Chart

Why?

When?

Monitor production processes.

How?

1. Select the labels and data.
2. Run the Cusum Chart
3. Evaluate the chart. Analyze special causes of sudden shifts.

Data

	A	B	C	D	E	F
1	Roll Number (Film Coating Weights)					
2	Position	Near Side	Middle	Far Side		
3	1	269	306	279		
4	2	274	275	302		
5	3	268	291	308		
6	4	280	277	306		
7	5	288	288	298		
8	6	278	288	313		
9	7	306	284	308		

Catches process changes or shifts more quickly than control charts can.

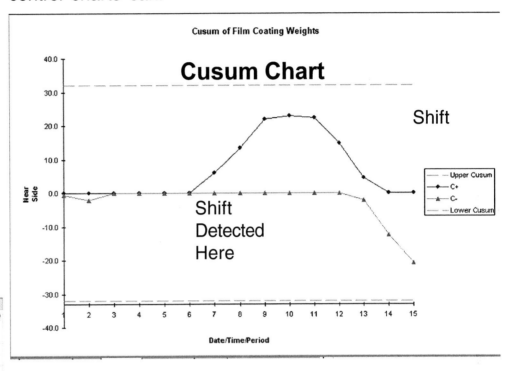

Cusum of Film Coating Weights

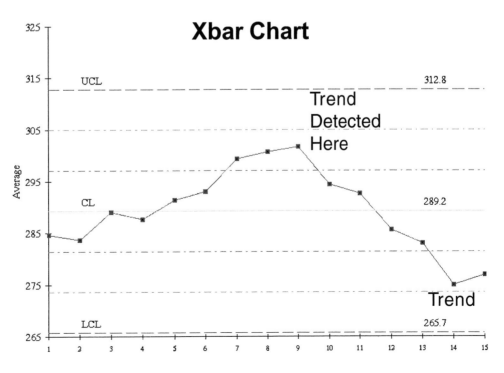

Film Coating Weights

EWMA Chart
Variable Data , Sample Size = 1-5/period

Why?

When?

Monitor process with only 1-5 samples of variable data per period.

The Exponentially Weighted Moving Average (EWMA) chart is a good alternative to an XmR chart when attempting to detect *small shifts* in performance. In this regard, the EWMA is similar to the Cusum chart.

How?

1. Select the labels and data.
2. Run the EWMA Chart
3. Evaluate the chart for shifts in performance (see trend at right).

Data

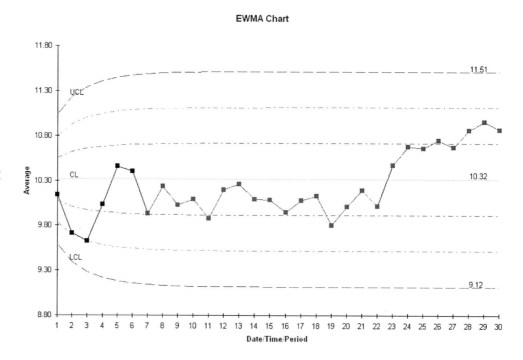

	A
1	Obs 1
2	9.45
3	7.99
4	9.29
5	11.66
6	12.16
7	10.18
8	8.04
9	11.46
10	9.2
11	10.34
12	9.03
13	11.47
14	10.51

Moving Average Chart
Variable Data, Sample Size = 1/period

Why?

When?

Monitor process with only 1-5 samples of variable data per period.

How?

1. Select the labels and data.
2. Run the Moving Average Chart
3. Evaluate the chart for shifts in performance. See trend at right; it's not quite as obvious as the EWMA.

Where the EWMA uses a *weighted* average, the moving average chart uses a simple, unweighted *moving* average.

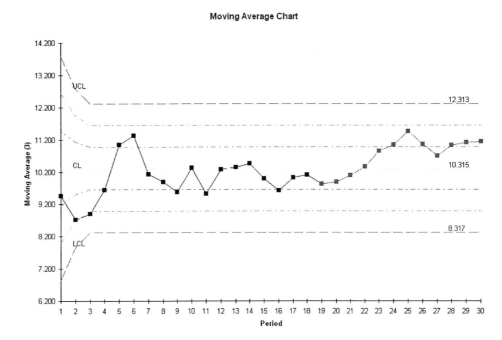

Moving Average Chart

Data

	A
1	Obs 1
2	9.45
3	7.99
4	9.29
5	11.66
6	12.16
7	10.18
8	8.04
9	11.46
10	9.2
11	10.34
12	9.03
13	11.47
14	10.51

Hotelling T² Chart
Variable Data, Sample Size = 2/period

Why?

When?
Monitor two factors simultaneously.

How?
1. Select the labels and data.
2. Run the Hotelling T2 Chart
3. Evaluate T22 (Range) chart. Analyze special causes of any instabilities.
4. Evaluate T21 (X) chart. Analyze special causes of any instabilities.

Data

	A	B
1	Large	Medium
2	5.4	93.6
3	3.2	92.6
4	5.2	91.7
5	3.5	86.9
6	2.9	90.4
7	4.6	92.1
8	4.4	91.5
9	5	90.3
10	8.4	85.1

Imagine for a moment that you are measuring the location of a hole drilled in a sheet of metal. It could be left or right, up or down. It's possible that both measurements, taken separately, could be stable and predictable, but the two together could have outliers. The T² chart helps evaluate two interacting measurements simultaneously.

Similar to the XmR, the Hotelling chart evaluates the covariances of the *ranges* between each of the two measures and the covariances of the actual data points. This gives two charts that are similar to the average and Range in the XmR.

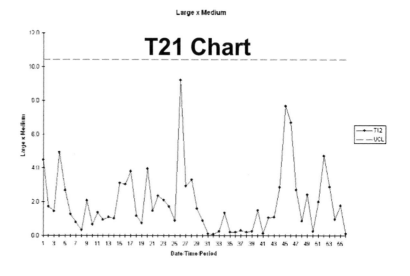

Large x Medium

T21 Chart

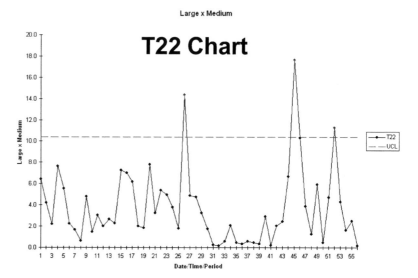

Large x Medium

T22 Chart

XmR Chart
Variable Data or Ratio, Sample Size = 1/period

Why?

Monitor and evaluate process performance using variable data when there is only one measurement per period.

When?

Monitor process with only one sample/ ratio of variable data per period.

How?

1. Select the labels and data.
2. Run the XmR Chart
3. Evaluate Range chart. Analyze special causes of any instabilities.
4. Evaluate X chart. Analyze special causes of any instabilities.

Data

Patient Falls/1000 days

	A	B
1	Month	Falls/1000
2	Jul-98	3.649635
3	Aug-98	4.481564
4	Sep-98	4.707327

X Chart Formulas

$$UCL = \overline{X} + E_2\overline{R}$$

$$CL = \overline{X} = \frac{\sum_{i=1,k} X_i}{k}$$

$$LCL = \overline{X} - E_2\overline{R}$$

Range Chart Formulas

$$UCL = D_4\overline{R}$$

$$CL = \overline{R} = \frac{\sum_{i=2,k} MR_i}{k-1}$$

$$MR_i = |X_i - X_{i-1}|$$

$$LCL = D_3\overline{R} = 0$$

X Chart (Ratio)

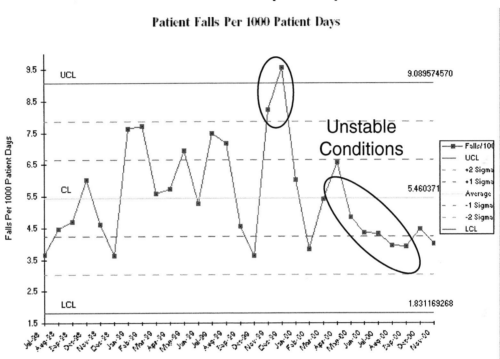

Patient Falls Per 1000 Patient Days

Moving Range Chart

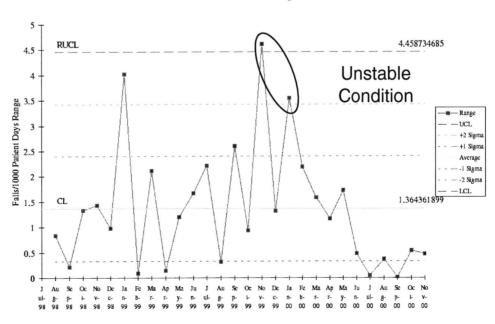

Patient Falls Range

XmR Trend Chart
Variable Data, Sample Size = 1/period

Why?

When?

Monitor process when you suspect there's an underlying trend.

How?

1. Select the labels and data.
2. Run the XmR Trend Chart
3. Evaluate Range chart. Analyze special causes of any instabilities.
4. Evaluate X chart. Analyze special causes of any instabilities.

Data

Fixed Costs ($000)

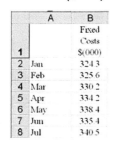

	A	B
1		Fixed Costs $(000)
2	Jan	324.3
3	Feb	325.6
4	Mar	330.2
5	Apr	334.2
6	May	338.4
7	Jun	335.4
8	Jul	340.5

	R Chart
UCL:	$D_4 \cdot \bar{R}$
CL:	$\bar{R} = \Sigma R_i/(k-1)$
	$R_i = X_{max} - X_{min}$
LCL:	$D_3 \cdot \bar{R}$
	X Chart
UCL:	$mt + b + A_2R$
CL:	$mt + b$
LCL:	$mt + b - A_2R$

Monitor and evaluate process performance using variable data when there is only one measurement per period, and the data may contain trends (e.g., inflation, increasing)

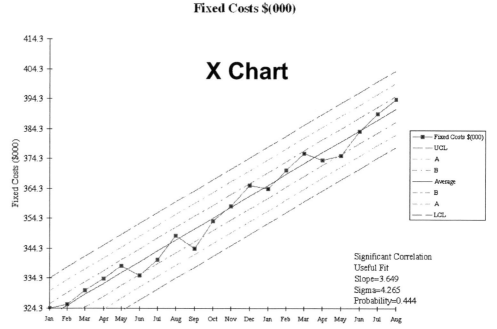

Fixed Costs $(000)

X Chart

Significant Correlation
Useful Fit
Slope=3.649
Sigma=4.265
Probability=0.444

What can you learn?

Significant correlation is a measure of the relationship between x and y.

Useful Fit is a measure of whether the relationship is useful. Can I make an assumption or prediction about y based on past history?

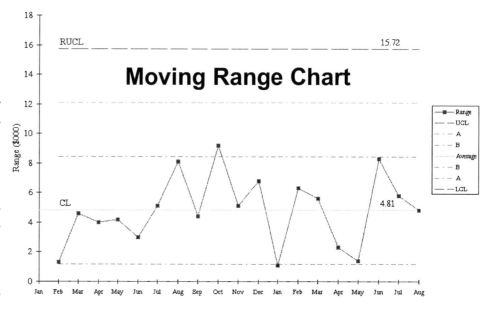

Fixed Costs ($000) Range

RUCL _____ 15.72

Moving Range Chart

CL _____ 4.81

XbarR Chart
Variable Data, Sample Size = 2-5/period

Why?

When?

Monitor process with only 2-5 samples of variable data per period.

How?

1. Select the labels and 2-5 samples.
2. Run the XbarR Charts
3. Analyze the Range chart for any special causes or instabilities.
4. Evaluate the X chart. Analyze special causes of any instabilities.

Monitor and evaluate process performance using time, length, weight, or cost when there are 2-5 samples per period

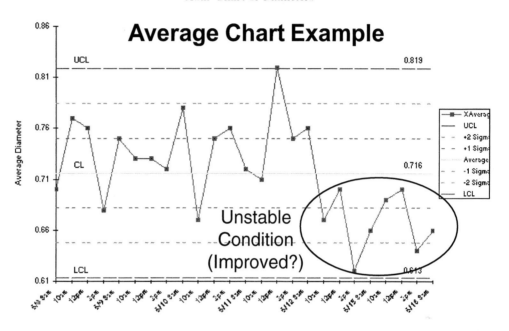

Xbar Chart of Diameters

Average Chart Example

Unstable Condition (Improved?)

Data

Diameters (5 samples)

	A	B	C	D	E	F
	Sample	1	2	3	4	5
6/8 8am	0.65	0.7	0.65	0.65	0.85
10am	0.75	0.85	0.75	0.85	0.65
12pm	0.75	0.8	0.8	0.7	0.75
2pm	0.6	0.7	0.7	0.75	0.65

X Chart Formulas

$$UCL = \overline{\overline{X}} + A_2\overline{R}$$

$$CL = \overline{\overline{X}} = \frac{\sum_{i=1,k}\overline{X}_i}{k}$$

$$LCL = \overline{\overline{X}} - A_2\overline{R}$$

Range Chart Formulas

$$UCL = D_4\overline{R}$$

$$CL = \overline{R} = \frac{\sum R_i}{k}$$

$$R_i = Max(X_i) - Min(X_i)$$

$$LCL = D_3\overline{R}$$

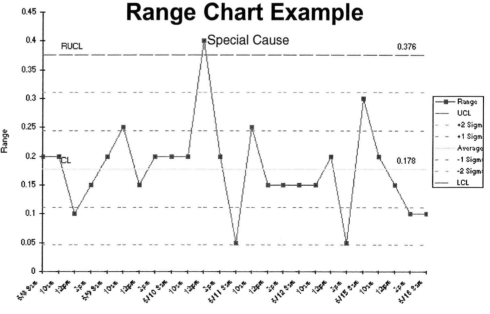

Range of Diameters

Range Chart Example

Special Cause

33

I-MR-R Chart
Variable Data, Sample Size = 2-5/period

Why?

When?

Monitor process to show "between" sample and "within" sample variation.

How?

1. Select the labels and 2-5 samples.
2. Run the I-MR-R Charts
3. Analyze the Range chart for any "within" subgroup special causes or instabilities.
4. Evaluate the MR chart. Analyze special causes of "between" subgroup variation.
5. Evaluate the X chart. Analyze special causes of any instabilities.

Monitor and evaluate process performance using time, length, weight, or cost when there are 2-or-more samples and you want to evaluate varation *within* and *between* subgroups.

X Chart

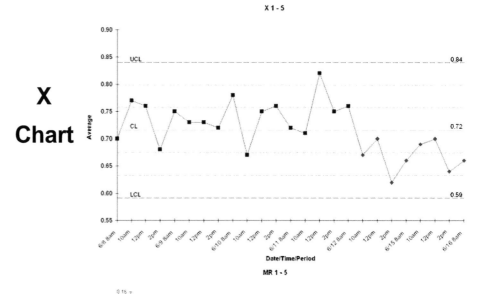

MR Chart

(between subgroup variation)

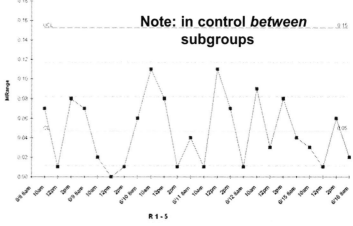

Note: in control *between* subgroups

R Chart

(within subgroup variation)

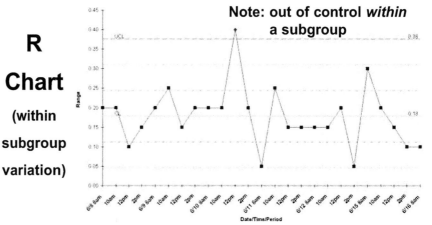

Note: out of control *within* a subgroup

Data

Diameters (5 samples)

	A	B	C	D	E	F
Sample	1	2	3	4	5	
6/8 8am	0.65	0.7	0.65	0.65	0.85	
10am	0.75	0.85	0.75	0.85	0.65	
12pm	0.75	0.8	0.8	0.7	0.75	
2pm	0.6	0.7	0.7	0.75	0.65	

XMedianR Chart
Variable Data, Sample Size = 1-5/period

When?

Monitor process with only 1-5 samples of variable data using the *median* instead of the average.

Monitor and evaluate process performance using time, length, weight, or cost when there are 2-10 samples per period

Median Chart Example

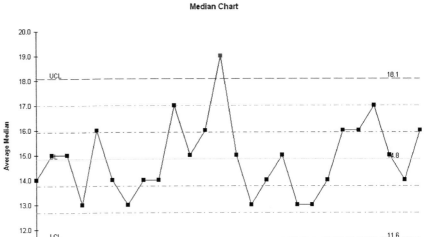

How?

1. Select the labels and 1-5 samples.
2. Run the XMedianR Charts
3. Analyze the Range chart for any special causes or instabilities.
4. Evaluate the Median chart. Analyze special causes of any instabilities.

Range Chart Example

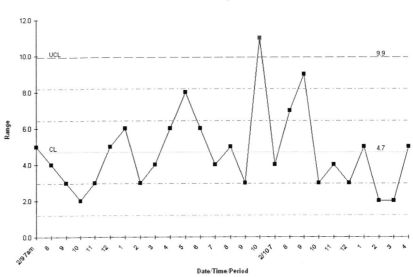

Data

Diameters (5 samples)

	A	B	C	D	E	F
1		x1	x2	x3	x4	x5
2	2/9 7am	16	14	13	12	17
3	8	16	15	13	15	17
4	9	16	13	16	15	15
5	10	15	13	13	13	14
6	11	16	15	16	14	17
7	12	13	13	14	17	18

Median Chart Formulas

$$UCL = X + A_2 R$$

$$CL = \bar{\bar{X}} = \frac{\sum \tilde{X}_i}{k}_{i=1,k}$$

$$LCL = \bar{\bar{X}} - A_2 \bar{R}$$

Range Chart Formulas

$$UCL = D_4 \bar{R}$$

$$CL = \bar{R} = \frac{\sum R_i}{k}$$

$$R_i = Max(X_i) - Min(X_i)$$

$$LCL = D_3 \bar{R}$$

$$\tilde{X}_k = \begin{cases} X^{\left(\frac{n+1}{2}\right)} & \text{If } n \text{ is odd} \\ \dfrac{X^{\left(\frac{n}{2}\right)} + X^{\left(\frac{n+2}{2}\right)}}{2} & \text{If } n \text{ is even} \end{cases}$$

XbarS Chart
Variable Data, Sample Size = 6-25/period

Why?

Monitor and evaluate process performance using time, length, weight, or cost when there are 6-25 samples per period

When?

Monitor process with 6 or more samples of variable data per period.

How?

1. Select the labels and data.
2. Run the XBarS Chart
3. Evaluate Range chart. Analyze special causes of any instabilities.
4. Evaluate X chart. Analyze special causes of any instabilities.

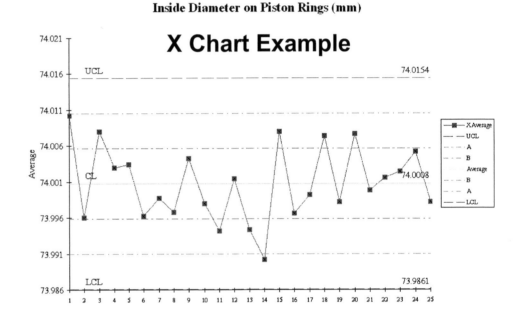

What can you learn?

These charts show that the process is stable and predictable with no special causes.

Data

Inside Diameters

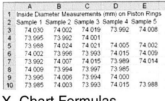

	A	B	C	D	E
1	Inside Diameter Measurements (mm) on Piston Rings				
2	Sample 1	Sample 2	Sample 3	Sample 4	Sample 5
3	74.030	74.002	74.019	73.992	74.008
4	73.995	73.992	74.001		
5	73.988	74.024	74.021	74.005	74.002
6	74.002	73.996	73.993	74.015	74.009
7	73.992	74.007	74.015	73.989	74.014
8	74.009	73.994	73.997	73.985	
9	73.995	74.006	73.994	74.000	
10	73.985	74.003	73.993	74.015	73.988

X Chart Formulas

$$UCL = \overline{\overline{X}} + A_3\overline{s}$$

$$CL = \overline{\overline{X}} = \frac{\sum_{i=1,k}\overline{X}_i}{k}$$

$$LCL = \overline{\overline{X}} - A_3\overline{s}$$

Range Chart Formulas

$$UCL = B_4\overline{s}$$

$$CL = \overline{s} = \frac{\sum s_i}{k}$$

$$LCL = B_3\overline{s}$$

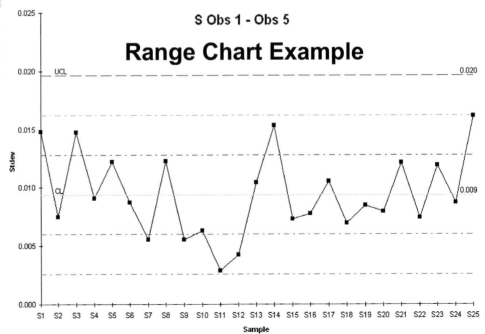

Anova
Analysis of Variance (Single factor)

Why?

When?

Evaluate tests of more than two samples of variable data.

How?

1. Select the labels and data.
2. Select Anova and Analysis (single factor).
3. Evaluate the average and standard deviation to determine the best fit.

Data

Hardwood concentration effects on paper tensile strength.

Tensile Strength of Paper (PSI)

Hardwood Concentration %	5%	10%	15%	20%
Obs1	7	12	14	19
Obs2	8	17	18	25
Obs3	15	13	19	22
Obs4	11	18	17	23
Obs5	9	19	16	18
Obs6	10	15	18	20

Tests the hypothesis that the means from several samples are equal (e.g., testing four different concentrations of an additive in a designed experiment to evaluate the effects). (For two-sample tests, use the t-Test.)

Anova: Single Factor

SUMMARY

Groups	Count	Sum	Average	Variance
5%	6	60	10	8
10%	6	94	15.66667	7.866667
15%	6	102	17	3.2
20%	6	127	21.16667	6.966667

ANOVA

rce of Varia	SS	df	MS	F	P-value	F crit
Between G	382.7917	3	127.5972	19.60521	3.59E-06	4.938215
Within Grc	130.1667	20	6.508333			
Total	512.9583	23				

Evaluation:

$P = 0.0000036 < \alpha = 0.01$

Reject that hypothesis that averages are equal

(i.e., Hardwood concentration <u>does</u> affect tensile strength)

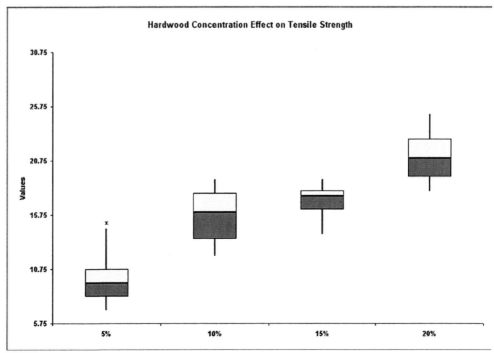

Hardwood Concentration Effect on Tensile Strength

Anova
Analysis of Variance (Two-factor)

Why?

When?

Evaluate tests of two factors using variable data.

How?

1. Select the labels and data.
2. Select Anova and Analysis (two-factor).
3. Evaluate the average and standard deviation to determine the best fit.

Data

Battery Material Type vs Operating Temperature.

Temperature	Material		
	1	2	3
15	130	150	138
15	74	159	168
15	155	188	110
15	180	126	160
70	34	136	174
70	80	106	150
70	40	122	120
70	75	115	139
125	20	25	96
125	82	58	82
125	70	70	104
125	58	45	60

Evaluate process performance when there are <u>more than one</u> sample for two factors (e.g., materials used in batteries vs operating temperature.)

ANOVA						
Source of Variation	SS	df	MS	F	P-value	F crit
Temperature	39119	2	19559.36	28.96769	1.91E-07	3.354131
Material	10684	2	5341.861	7.911372	0.001976	3.354131
Interaction	9614	4	2403.444	3.559535	0.018611	2.727766
Within	18231	27	675.213			
Total	77647	35				

Evaluation:

$P_{temp} = 0.00 < \alpha = 0.05$
$P_{material} = 0.002 < \alpha = 0.05$
$P_{Interaction} = 0.02 < \alpha = 0.05$

Significant interaction between material types and temperature.

Material Type 3 performs best in all temperatures.

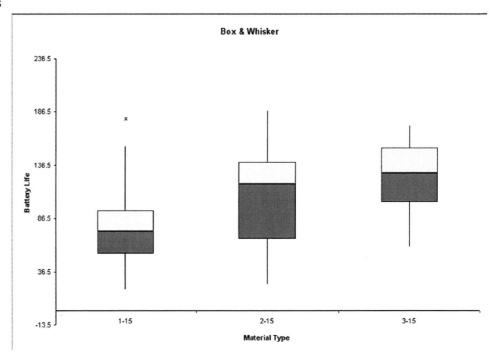

© 2010 Jay Arthur

QI Macros Example Book

Chi-Squared (X^2)

Why?

When?

Evaluate differences using Chi-squared distribution and test.

How?

1. Select the labels and data.
2. Select Anova and Analysis (Chi-Squared).
3. Evaluate the *p* value. Is it less than your confidence level?

	A	B	C
10		Men	Women
11	Agree	58	35
12	Neutral	11	25
13	Disagree	10	23

Evaluate two sets of data to determine if they are statistically different. Suppose that you've asked groups of men and women a question and you want to know if there is a difference between their answers.

	A	B	C	D	E	F
1		Men	Women	Total	Chi-Sq	16.164
2	Agree	58	35	93	*p*	0.0003
3	Neutral	11	25	36		
4	Disagree	10	23	33		
5	Total	79	83	162		

In this case, you would expect the number of men and women to be about the same. They aren't, but are they statistically different?

The *p* value of 0.0003 says that at the 0.005 level (99.5% confidence), the responses are different.

F- Test

Why?

When?

Evaluate the equality of two or more sets of data based on standard deviation. In the example below, the standard deviations are considered equal.

Evaluate if the standard deviations of two populations are equal.

	A	B	C	D	E
1	**Recipe1**	**Recipe2**	F-Test Two-Sample for Variances		
2	3067	3200			
3	2730	2777		*Recipe2*	*Recipe1*
4	2840	2623	Mean	2895.6	2867.8
5	2913	3044	Variance	51713.3	16923.7
6	2789	2834	Observations	5	5
7			df	4	4
8			F	3.055673	
9			P(F<=f) one-tail	0.152407	
10			F Critical one-tail	6.388234	

How?

1. Select the labels and data.
2. Select Anova and Analysis (F-test).
3. If the F value is less than F-Critical, the standard deviations are equal.

In Excel, the Analysis Toolpak only gives the correct answer when the mean of the first sample is greater than the mean of the second. That's why Recipe 1 and 2 are reversed.

Data

	A	B
1	**Recipe1**	**Recipe2**
2	3067	3200
3	2730	2777
4	2840	2623
5	2913	3044
6	2789	2834

Regression Analysis

Why?
When?

Evaluate correlations.

Evaluate the correlation (i.e., cause-effect) between two or more sets of data. Regression arrives at an equation to predict performance based on each of the inputs.

How?

1. Select the labels and data.
2. Select Anova and Analysis (Regression).
3. Evaluate the R-squared (>0.80 is a good fit).
4. Develop $y = b + mx$ model of performance.

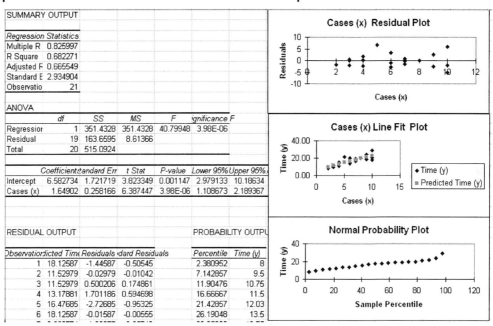

Data

Cases vs delivery time.

Delivery Time Data - E

Time (y)	Cases (x)
16.68	7
11.50	3
12.03	3
14.88	4
13.75	6
18.11	7
8.00	2
17.83	7
21.50	5
21.00	10
13.50	4
19.75	6
24.00	9
29.00	10
15.35	6
19.00	7
9.50	3
17.90	10
18.75	9
19.83	8
10.75	4

Evaluation:

R squared < 0.80 (poor fit)
R squared > 0.80 (good fit)

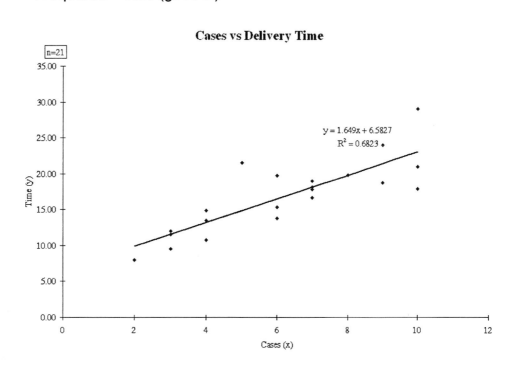

t-Test
Assuming Equal Variances

Why?

When?

Evaluate tests of two samples of variable data.

How?

1. Select the labels and data.
2. Select Anova and Analysis (t-Test).
3. Evaluate the test statistic (t Stat) to evaluate hypotheses.

Data

How do catalysts effect the yield of a chemical process.

t-Test data	
Catalyst 1	Catalyst2
91.5	89.19
94.18	90.95
92.18	90.46
95.39	93.21
91.79	97.19
89.07	97.04
94.72	91.07
89.21	92.75

Test "hypotheses" about the <u>means of two distinct samples</u> from a designed experiment:

Null Hypothesis:
Average(population1) = Average(population2)
Accept if: -t two-tail < tstat < +t two-tail

Alternate Hypothesis:
Average(population1) <> Average(population2)

t-Test: Two-Sample Assuming Equal Variances		
	Catalyst 1	Catalyst2
Mean	92.255	92.7325
Variance	5.68831	8.90099
Observations	8	8
Pooled Variance	7.29465	
Hypothesized Mean Difference	0	
df	14	
t Stat	-0.35359	
P(T<=t) one-tail	0.36446	
t Critical one-tail	1.76131	
P(T<=t) two-tail	0.72891	
t Critical two-tail	2.14479	

Evaluation:
t_0 = -2.14479 < -0.35359 < +2.14479
P two-tail = 0.72891 > α = 0.05
Can't reject that hypothesis that averages are equal
(so accept that the averages are equal for both catalysts)

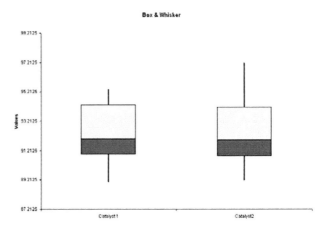

Box & Whisker

Six Sigma Templates

To automate all of your improvement documentation,
get *The QI Macros For Microsoft Excel.*
If you have the QI Macros you can access these
templates under the Fill in the Blanks Templates.

Action Plan

Why?

When?

After problem solving to identify a plan for implementing changes.

How?

1. Identify *what* needs to be done to revise strategy, process, organization, and technology to implement the change.
2. Provide more detail about *how* it will be accomplished.
3. Identify who is responsible for completing each piece of the change
4. Identify due dates for the change.

A good Six Sigma implementation plan will identify:

- **What** activities to implement
- **How** to do them
- **Who** will do them
- **When** they will be started and completed
- **How** they will be measured

	A	B	C	D	E
1				**Action Plan**	
2	Type	What	How	Who	When
3	Strategy	Investigate Fast Track Awards based on Exam while awaiting evidence	Identify legal issues to be resolved.	Legal Review	1-Oct-01
4	People	Training on streamlined process			1-Nov-01
5	Process	Develop Merit Criteria for Exam Request (80% of cases)	Evaluate current case load to identify common criteria.	Lynn/Sharon	1-Oct-01
6		Implement Streamlined Process	Develop staffing and implementation Plan	John/Lynn	1-Nov-01
7	Technology	Increase % of records stored electronically		Steve	1-Jan-02

Affinity Diagram

Why?

When?

To organize large, complex, or chaotic groups of information (e.g., customer requirements).

How?

1. **State the issue** to be examined in broad terms

2. **Generate and record ideas** using Post-it™ notes.

3. **Arrange the cards in related groupings**.

4. **Duplicate cards** as required.

5. **Choose a word or phrase that captures the intent of each group** and place it at the top as a header card.

The affinity diagram helps brainstorm and organize the team's thoughts when the issues are large and complex

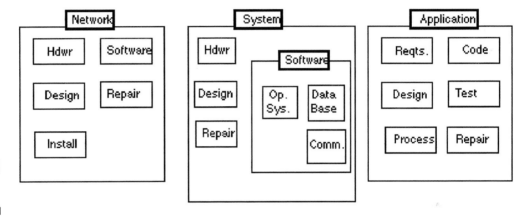

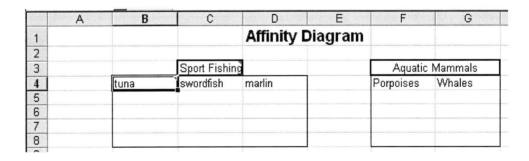

Arrow Diagram
(Critical Path Analysis)

Why?   Plan and project manage complex tasks.

When?

To develop a plan for a complex project and identify the critical path.

How?

1. Identify all of the tasks required to complete the project.

2. Put the tasks in order.

3. Assign times to each task.

4. Calculate shortest schedule.

5. Assign early and late start dates to each task.

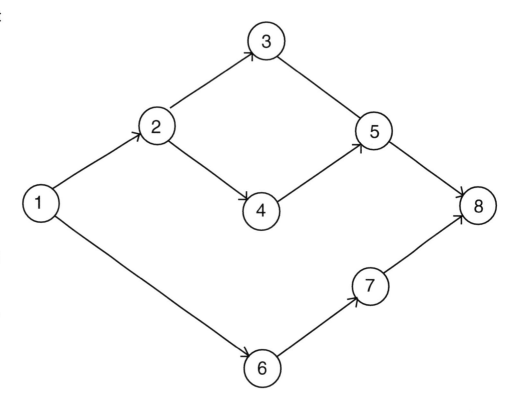

Balanced Scorecard

Why?

When?

To align corporate objectives using Key Performance Indicators (KPIs)

To be successful, companies need to measure and monitor four main results:

- **Financial** - profit
- **Customer Satisfaction**
- **Quality** - speed, quality, cost
- **Growth**

How?

1. Identify financial goals and measures.

2. Identify customer satisfaction measures.

3. Identify quality objects for speed, quality and cost.

4. Identify growth goals.

5. Measure and monitor progress. Reward employees based on performance of these Key Performance Indicators.

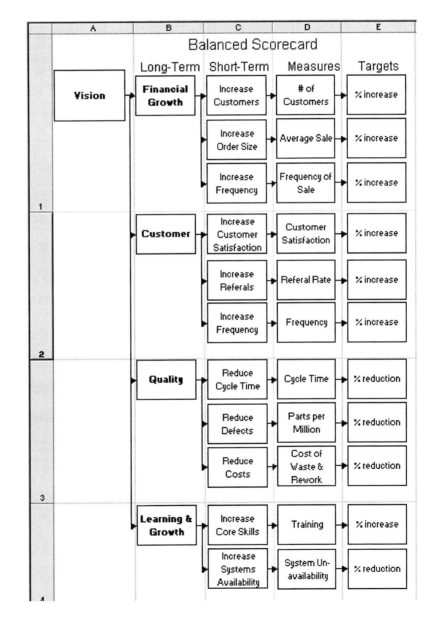

Block Diagram

Why?

When?

When designing systems that need extra reliability (e.g., the space shuttle has 5 redundant computers, one is programmed separately).

How?

1. Lay out a diagram of parallel and serial components

2. Identify probability of failure of each component (value 0-1).

3. Calculate parallel probabilities. (a+b-a*b)

4. Multiply serial component probabilities (a*b)

5. Use parallel parts to increase reliability.

To design reliability of systems. Use block diagrams for equipment and flow charts for processes. There are three types of block diagrams:

- **System** - physical relationship of major system components
- **Functional** - Categorize system components according to the function they provide.
- **Reliability** - depicts the effect of a component failure on the system's function.

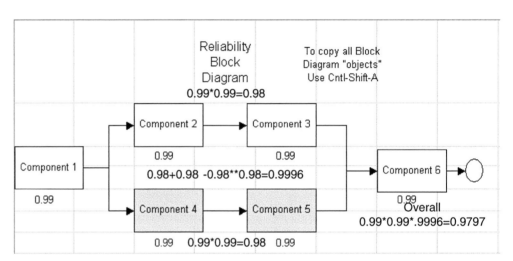

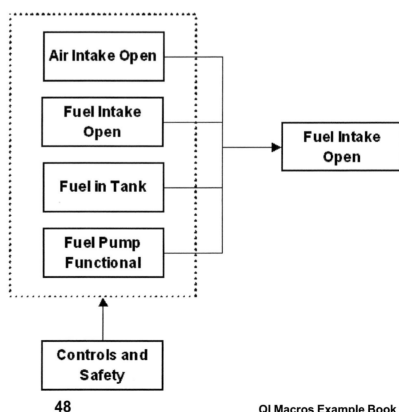

Control Chart Dashboards

Why?

When?

When reporting several measures to leadership.

How?

1. Open up the Xmr or c, p, u, np chart dashboard.

2. Input or cut and paste your data into the data input sheet.

3. Click on the chart sheet You will see charts for the first data set.

4. Click on the arrows to view charts for each data set.

5. Click on the Create Dashboard icon to create a dashboard with each chart.

To show control charts for several measures on the same worksheet. For more detail see qimacros.com/qiwizard/control-chart-dashboard.html

Each dashboard has an instruction sheet, a data input sheet and a sheet for each available control chart and a run chart.

◄◄ ◄ ► ►◄ \ **Instructions** / Data Sheet / XmR AverageR / XmR MedianR / Run Chart /

Data Input Sheet

	A	B	C	D
1	X Axis Labels	Chart Title 1	Chart Title 2	Chart Title 3
2	1	75	33.75	216
3	2	74	33.05	290
4	3	82	34.00	236
5	4	69	33.81	228
6	5	78	33.46	244
7	6	83	34.02	210
8	7	76	33.68	139
9	8	67	33.27	310
10	9	65	33.49	240
11	10	63	33.20	211

Chart Sheet

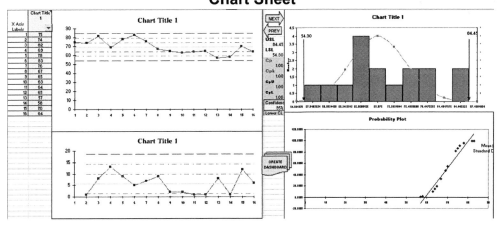

Control Chart Dashboard

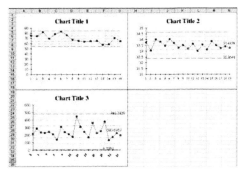

Control Plan

Why?

When?

Design for Six Sigma

How?

1. Identify production control plan and part number.

2. Identify characteristics of the process or product on which variable or attribute data will be collected.

3. For details, see TS16949 or QS-9000 APQP (Advanced Product Quality Planning guide).

Aid the manufacturing of quality products by using a structured approach to identify and implement value-added controls to minimize process and product variation.

CONTROL PLAN

Prototype	Prelaunch	X Production	Key Contact/Phone	Date(Orig)	Date (Rev.)
Control Plan Number	001		Jay Arthur 888-468-1537	1/12/2002	10/21/2002
Part Number/Latest Change Level	225212 11/2/02		Core Team Product Development	Customer Eng. Approval/Date	
Part Name/Description	Plastic Injection Molded Grill		Supplier/Plant Approval/Date	Customer Quality Approval/Date	
Supplier/Plant		Supplier Code 0123	Other Approval/Date (If Req'd)	Other Approval/Date	

Part/ Process Number	Process Name/ Operation Description	Machine, Device, Jig, Tools, for Mfg.	Characteristics — No.	Characteristics — Product	Characteristics — Process	Special Char Class	Product/Process Specification/ Tolerance	Evaluation/ Measurement Technique	Methods — Size	Methods — Freq.	Control Method	Reaction Plan
3	Plastic Injection Molding											
		Machine No 1-5	18	Appearance			Free of Blemishes	Visual Inspection	100%	Contin uous	100% Inspection	Notify Supervisor
				No Blemishes			Flow Lines	1st piece buy-off			Checksheet	Adjust/ re-check
							sink markes	1st piece buy-off			Checksheet	Adjust/ re-check
		Machine No. 1-5	19	Mounting Hole Loc.			Hole "X" Location	Fixture #10	1st Piece	buy-off per run	Checksheet	Adjust/ re-check
							25 +/- 1mm		5 pcs	hr	XbarR	Quarantine and adjust
		Machine No. 1-5	20	Dimension			Gap 3+/- 5mm	Fixture #10	1st piece	buy-off per run	Checksheet	Adjust/ re-check
		Fixture #10	21	Perimeter fit			Gap 3+/-5mm	Check gap to fixture 4 locations	5 pcs	hr	XbarR	Quarantine and adjust
		Machine No. 1-5	22		Set-up of mold machine		See attached set-up card	Review of set-up card and machine settings	Each set-up	1st piece buy off	Adjust and reset machine

Cost Benefit Analysis

Identify the potential costs of implementing a countermeasure and the potential benefit

Why?

When?

After problem solving to identify a plan for implementing changes.

How?

1. Identify the resources required to implement the countermeasure:
   - People
   - Money
   - Time

2. Identify the tangible and intangible benefits of implementing the countermeasure (based on the data gathered in step 1).

3. Is the return worth the investment?

	A	B	C
1	**Cost/Benefit Analysis**		
2			
3	**Countermeasures**	**Cost**	**Benefit**
4	Upgrade software to new requirements	$25,000	$250,000/month
5			
6			
7			
8			
9			
10			
11			
12			
13			
14			
15			
16			
17			
18			
19			
20			
21			
22			
23			
24			

Cost of Quality Analysis

Why?

When?

During laser-focus of improvement effort. (Is this problem worth solving?)

How?

1. Identify each step in the Fix-it process.
2. Assign a time in minutes to each task and a loaded rate.
3. Identify any material costs associated with each step.
4. Identify any external costs of this failure.
5. Identify any lost opportunity, asset, or business costs.
6. Set a target for reducing the error (e.g., 50%)
7. Estimate the total cost of achieving this level of prevention.
8. Evaluate ROI and payback period.

Evaluate the true costs of a defect or error. This is the foundation of making a business case for the change.

	A	B	C	D	E	F	G
1	**Cost of Quality Worksheet**						
2	**Problem Description:** Service Order Errors					**Type:** Internal	
3	**Tasks**	**Average Hours/ Task**	**Hourly Rate**	**Cost of Task**	**Material Costs**	**External Failure Cost**	**Total Cost of Non-Conformance**
4	1. Analyze Service Order Error	0.17	$60	$10.00	$3.00	$0.00	$13.00
5	2. Fix Error **1.**	**2.** 0.08	$60	$5.00 **3.**	$3.00 **4.**	$0.00	$8.00
6	3. Admin	0.05	$60	$3.00	$0.00	$0.00	$3.00
7	4. Billing Costs Due to Error	0.03	$60	$2.00		$0.00	$2.00
8	**Total Cost Per Failure**						$26.00
9	Service Order Errors/year						221,000
10	1. Lost Opportunity Costs					$0.00	$0.00
11	2. Lost Assets Costs **5.**					$0.00	$0.00
12	3. Lost Business Costs					$0.00	$0.00
13	Additional Failure Costs						$0.00
14	**Annual Failure Cost**						$5,746,000.00
15						Customer or	
16	Basic tasks to fix the problem	Average min/60	Loaded rate	Calculated cost	Expenses	Employee found	Total
17							
18	**Return on Investment and Payback**						
19	**6.**	**Target Reduction**				50%	$2,873,000
20	**7.**	**Prevention Costs**					$225,000
21	**8.**	ROI					$13:$1
22		**Payback Period (days)**					17

Types of Costs

Internal Failure Costs:
- Scrap
- Rework
- Failure analysis
- Reinspecting and retesting rework
- Avoidable losses (e.g., overfill)
- Downgrading price due to quality

Appraisal Costs:
- Inspection and test
- Product quality audits
- Measurement system analysis

Prevention Costs:
- Planning
- Statistical Process Control
- Training
- Supplier evaluations

External Failure Costs:
- Warranty Charges
- Complaints and adjustments
- Allowances and concessions

Countermeasures Matrix

Why?

When?

After problem solving to identify a plan for implementing your changes.

Identify and prioritize the countermeasures required to reduce or eliminate the root causes. (This is one of many possible "prioritization" matrices you might use to evaluate alternatives. See also Pugh Concept Selection.)

How?

1. Get the problem statement from your fishbone diagram.
2. For each root cause, identify one to three countermeasures (what to do).
3. Rank the effectiveness of each countermeasure (Low, Medium, or High).
4. Identify the specific actions (how to do it).
5. Rank the feasibility (time, cost) of each specific action.
6. Decide which specific actions to implement.

	Root Cause	Countermeasure	Feasibility	Specific Actions	Effectiveness	Overall	Action (Who?)	Value ($/week)
Problem Statement:	From October to November, server availability averaged 100,000 minutes of downtime per week.							
	Corrupted Password files	Upgrade to latest operating system	4	Develop and implement installation plan across server environment.	5	20	MI S	$14,667
	Application Design problems	Maintenance release of applications	4	Identify changes in design and implement changes	4	16	IT	$3,667
						0		

Feasibility: 1-low, 5-high
1-Expensive & Difficult to implement
5-Inexpensive and easy to implement

Effectiveness: 1-low, 5-high
1-Not very effective
5-Very Effective

Cp and Cpk Worksheet

Why?

When?

Capability Analysis

How?

1. Identify characteristics of each part to be measured.

2. Specify Upper and Lower Specification Limits.

3. Enter measurements in the data section as they are selected.

$$Cp = \frac{(USL - LSL)}{6\hat{\sigma}}$$

$$CpU = \frac{(USL - \overline{X})}{3\hat{\sigma}}$$

$$CpL = \frac{(\overline{X} - LSL)}{3\hat{\sigma}}$$

$$Cpk = Min(CpU, CpL)$$

Aid the manufacturing of quality products by measuring capability (Cp, Cpk, Pp, and Ppk). Cp (process capability) should be close to Pp (process performance). Similarly, Cpk should be close to Ppk. Otherwise, the process is unstable and should be evaluated with control charts.

	A	B	C	D	E	F	G	H	I
1						Supplier			
2	Part Number	12345			Your Name Here				6/7/2007
3	Characteristic	Characteristic 1	Characteristic 2	Characteristic 3	Characteristic 4	Characteristic 5	Characteristic 6	Characteristic 7	Characteristic 8
4	Target	1.500							
5	+Tol	0.250							
6	-Tol	0.250							
7	USL	1.750	0.000	0.000	0.000	0.000	0.000	0.000	0.000
8	LSL	1.250	0.000	0.000	0.000	0.000	0.000	0.000	0.000
9	AVE	1.523							
10	MAX	1.560	0.000	0.000	0.000	0.000	0.000	0.000	0.000
11	MIN	1.470	0.000	0.000	0.000	0.000	0.000	0.000	0.000
12	USL-LSL	0.500	0.000	0.000	0.000	0.000	0.000	0.000	0.000
13	σ	0.047							
14	σest	0.040							
15	Cp	2.089							
16	Cpk	1.894							
17	CpU	1.894							
18	CpL	2.284							
19	Pp	1.763							
20	Ppk	1.599							
21	PpU	1.599							
22	PpL	1.928							
23									
24	Sample #	Characteristic 1	Characteristic 2	Characteristic 3	Characteristic 4	Characteristic 5	Characteristic 6	Characteristic 7	Characteristic 8
25	1	1.470							
26	2	1.540							
27	3	1.560							

Design of Experiments

Why?

When?

During Design for Six Sigma or to find optimal values for interacting factors.

How?

1. Determine objectives, potential causes, and factors (usually 2,3,or 4 factors).

2. Select experimental factors, identify potential interactions, and levels (+/-,high/low)

3. Choose appropriate design (4, 8, or 16 trials) and randomize sequence of trials

4. Run the experiment

5. Analyze the data to determine interactions and best factor levels

6. Verify results

The purpose of DOE is to quickly and efficiently discover the optimum conditions that produce top quality. Trial-and-error is the slowest method of discovering these optimal conditions and usually misses the effects of various interactions. DOE significantly reduces the time and trials necessary to discover the best combination of factors to produce the desired level of quality and robustness.

	A	B	C	D	E	F	G	H	I	J
1	Design of Experiments				L4					
2	Factor	Factor Name			Level 1		Level 2			
3	A	Die Temperature			Room temp		200 degrees			
4	B	Pour Time			6 sec		12 sec			
5	AB	Die Temperature X Pour Time								
6										
7	Design	Factors			Trial Responses					
8	Trial	A	B	AB	1	2	3	Average		
9	1	-	-	+	122.3	121.5	121.9	121.90		
10	2	-	+	-	128.5	129	128.2	128.57		
11	3	+	-	-	127.3	127.9	127.8	127.67		
12	4	+	+	+	125.8	125.2	126.2	125.73		
13				Average	125.98	125.90	126.03	125.97		
14		(1)	3	2						
15	Interactions		(2)	1						
16				(3)						
17				Pour Time Low	Pour Time High					
18	Low (-)	125.23	124.78	121.90	128.57					
19	High (+)	126.70	127.15	127.67	125.73					
20										
21	Anova	Factor			df	SS	MS	F	Effect	Contrast
22	Source	Die Temperature			1	6.45	6.45333	37.9608	1.5	8.80
23		Pour Time			1	16.80	16.8033	98.8431	2.4	14.20
24		Die Temperature X Pour Time			1	55.47	55.47	326.294	-4.3	-25.80
25		Error			8	1.36	0.170			
26		Total			11	80.09				

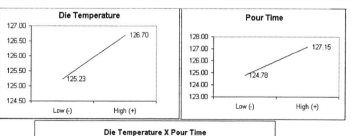

Slope of line shows there is an effect caused by both factors.

(Flat line = no effect.)

Optimal solution lies at intersection of "confounding" factors (e.g., higher temp, longer pour time).

Fault Tree Analysis
(Reliability)

Why?

When?

After problem solving to identify plan for implementing changes.

How?

1. Taking a failure event that occurred, analyze that event (ask why?)

2. List failures, events, or conditions that had to exist to cause the failure.

3. Use logic symbols to connect the causes (e.g., this *and* that cause the failure.)

Fault trees take reliability block diagrams one step further by adding logic symbols (and/or) to connect the blocks. (Similar to root cause analysis.)

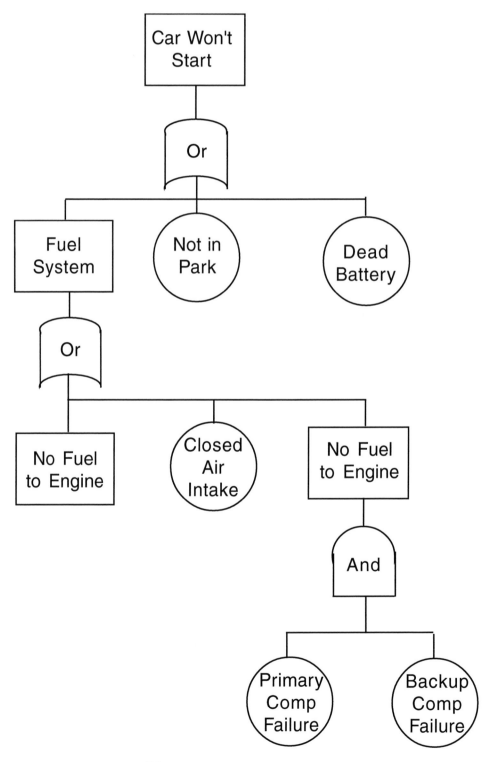

Flow Chart

Why?

When?

Before Value-Added Analysis or after improvement.

How?

1. Start with identifying customer needs and end with satisfying them.

2. Separate the process into areas of responsibility

3. Use square Post-it™ notes to lay out activities and decisions

4. Place activities under the appropriate area of responsibility.

5. Identify internal and external quality indicators.

Define the <u>existing</u> or improved process as a starting point for stabilization

Flowchart symbols:

⬭	Start/End	Customer initiated	
▭	Activity	Adding value to the (verb–noun)	product or service
◇	Decision	Choosing among two or more alternatives	
→	Arrow	Showing the flow and	transition
◯	Indicator	Process or Quality Indicator	

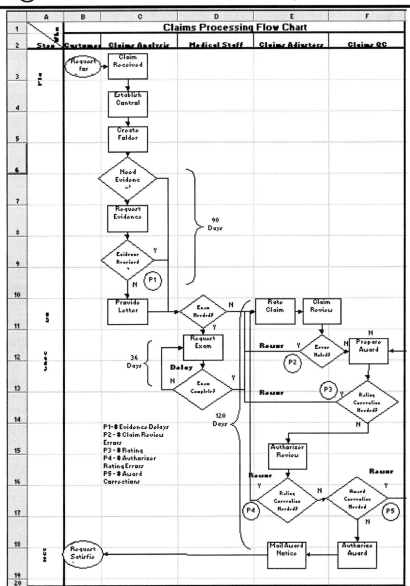

EMEA (Process FMEA)
Error Modes and Effects Analysis

Recognize and evaluate potential failures of a process; Identify actions to prevent the failure; and document the process.

Why?
When?

1. New process/ design
2. Modified process/ design
3. Existing process applied in a new environment

How?

1. Flowchart the process
2. Describe process and function
3. List each potential failure mode
4. Describes effects of each type of failure
5. Rank severity of failure
6. Classify any special characteristics
7. List every potential cause or failure mechanism for each failure mode.
8. Estimate the likelihood of occurrence of each failure/ cause
9. List prevention/ detection controls
10. Rank detection
11. Identify actions to reduce severity, occurrence, and detection.

Process FMEA (EMEA)						AIAG Third Edition									
Insert here	Process Responsibility:			Insert here		EMEA Number	Insert # here								
sub	Key Date:				1/1/2003	Page		1 of 1							
2003-						Prepared by:	who								
who						EMEA Date	1/1/2003				Action Results				
Potential Failure Mode	Potential Effect(s) of Failure	S e v	C l a s s	Potential Cause(s) / Mechanism(s) of Failure	O c c u r	Current Process Controls Prevention	Current Process Controls Detection	D e t e c t	R. P. N.	Recommended Action(s)	Responsibility & Target Completion Date	Actions Taken	S e v	O c c u r	D e t e c t	R. P. N.
Describe how product or process could potentially fail.	What the internal or external customer might notice or experience: noise, impaired function.			Describe how the failure could occur described in terms of what chan be corrected or controlled: improper action.		Process methods and controls to prevent failure.	Process methods and controls to detect failure.			Changes to reduce severity, occurrence, and detection ratings.	Name of organization or individual and target completion date	Actions and actual completion date				
									0							0
									0							0
									0							0
									0							0
									0							0
									0							0

Severity of Effect:	Occurrence Rating	Detection:
1. None	1. Remote < .01/1000	1. Very High
2. Very Minor	2. Low - 0.1/1000	2. Very High
3. Minor	3. Low - 0.5/1000	3. High
4. Very Low	4. Moderate - 1/1000	4. Moderately High
5. Low	5. Moderate - 2/1000	5. Moderate
6. Moderate	6. Moderate - 5/1000	6. Low
7. High	7. High - 10/1000	7. Very Low
8. Very High	8. High - 20/1000	8. Remote
9. Hazardous with warning	9. Very High 50/1000	9. Very Remote
10. Hazardous w/o warning	10. Very High >100/100	10. Almost Impossible

RPN= Risk Priority Number

Sample

Process FMEA (EMEA)						AIAG Third Edition									
Item/Process	Process Responsibility:					EMEA Number									
Subsystem	Key Date:					Page		of							
Model Years						Prepared by:									
Core Team:						EMEA Date					Action Results				
Process Function Requirements	Potential Failure Mode	Potential Effect(s) of Failure	S e v	C l a s s	Potential Cause(s) / Mechanism(s) of Failure	O c c u r	Current Process Controls Prevention	Current Process Controls Detection	D e t e c t	R. P. N.	Recommended Action(s)	Responsibility & Target Completion Date	Actions Taken	S e v	O c c u r	D e t e c t	R. P. N.
Manual application of wax inside door	Insufficient wax coverage over specified surface	Deteriorated life of the door leading to:	7		Manually inserted spray head not inserted far enough	8		Visual check each hour for film thickness and coverage	5	280	Add positive depth stop to sprayer Automate spraying	MFG Engineering	Stop added Rejected due to complexity	7	2	5	70
		Unsatisfactory appearance due to rust	7		spray heads clogged	5	Test spray pattern	Visual check each hour for film thickness and coverage	5	175	Use DOE on viscosity vs temperature vs pressure	MFG Engineering	Temp and press limits determined and controls installed	7	1	5	35
		Impaired function of interior door hardware	7		spray head deformed	2	Preventive maintenance	Visual check each hour for film thickness and coverage	5	70	None	MFG Engineering					0
					Spray time insufficient	8		Operator instructions and lot sampling (10 doors/shift)	7	392	Install spray timer	Maintenance	Automatic spray timer installed. Operator starts timer controls shut off.	7	1	7	49
										0							0

FMEA
Failure Modes and Effects Analysis

Why?

Recognize and evaluate potential failures of a product or process; Identify actions to prevent the failure; and document the process.

When?

1. New process/ design
2. Modified process/ design
3. Existing process applied in new environment

How?

1. Enter part name
2. List each potential failure mode
3. Describes effects of each type of failure
4. Rank severity of failure
5. Classify any special characteristics
6. List every potential cause or failure mechanism for each failure mode.
7. Estimate the likelihood of occurrence of each failure/ cause
8. List prevention/ detection controls
9. Rank detection
10. Identify actions to reduce severity, occurrence, and detection.

Failure Mode and Effects Analysis — AIAG Third Edition

System:	Design Responsibility:			FMEA Number												
Subsystem	Key Date:			Page		of										
Component				Prepared by:												
Model:				FMEA Date:												
Core Team:												**Action Results**				

Item/Part Function	Potential Failure Mode	Potential Effect(s) of Failure	Sev	Class	Potential Cause(s) / Mechanism(s) of Failure	Occ	Current Design Controls Prevention	Current Design Controls Detection	Det	R.P.N.	Recommended Action(s)	Responsibility & Target Completion Date	Actions Taken	Sev	Occ	Det	R.P.N.

What are the Functions, Features, or Requirements?

What are the Effects?

How bad is it?

How often does it happen?

What can go wrong?
1. No function
2. Degraded function
3. Unintended function

What are the Causes?

How can this be detected and prevented?

What can be done?
Changes to:
1. Design
2. Process
3. Controls
4. Documentation

Severity of Effect:	Occurrence Rating	Detection:	Detection:	RPN= Risk Priority Number
1. None	1. Remote < .01/1000	1. Almost Certain	1. Almost Certain	
2. Very Minor	2. Low - 0.1/1000	2. Very High	2. Very High	

Sample

Failure Mode and Effects Analysis — AIAG Third Edition

System:	Design Responsibility:			FMEA Number												
Subsystem	Key Date:			Page		of										
Component				Prepared by:												
Model:				FMEA Date:												
Core Team:												**Action Results**				

Item/Part Function	Potential Failure Mode	Potential Effect(s) of Failure	Sev	Class	Potential Cause(s) / Mechanism(s) of Failure	Occ	Current Design Controls Prevention	Current Design Controls Detection	Det	R.P.N.	Recommended Action(s)	Responsibility & Target Completion Date	Actions Taken	Sev	Occ	Det	R.P.N.
Front Door LH HBHX-0000-A	Corroded interior lower door pannels	Deteriorated life of door leading to:	7		Upper edge of protective wax application specified for inner door panels is too low	6		Vehicle general durability test veh. T-118	7	294	Add laboratory accelerated corrosion testing	A. Tate-Body Engineering Corrosion testing	Based on test results, upper edge spec raised 125mm	7	2	2	28
		1. Unsatisfactory appearance due to rust through point over time	7		Insufficient wax thickness specified	4		Vehicle general durability testing	7	196	Conduct DOE on xax thickness	A.Tate	Thickness is adequate.	7	2	2	28
		2. Impaired function of interior door hardware	7		Insufficient room between panels for spray head access	4		Drawing evaluation of spray head access	4	112	Add team evaluation using design aid buck and spary head	Body Engineering	Evaluation showed adequate access.	7	1	1	7
										0							0

Force Field Analysis

Why?

Identify the potential roadblocks and problems associated with implementing a countermeasure

When?

After selecting countermeasures and before implementation.

How?

1. Brainstorm the <u>existing</u> forces acting against the introduction of a countermeasure.

2. Brainstorm the <u>existing</u> forces that can help overcome these barriers. Match them to the barriers.

3. Use the unmatched forces acting against implementation to develop the action plan.

	A	B	C
1		**Force Field Analysis**	
2		**Forces**	
3	**Countermeasures**	**For**	**Against**
4	Six Sigma	Customers want better products	Resistance to new "programs"
5		Employees want to improve the business	Math anxiety
6		Rising costs	Time constraints
7		Shrinking profits	Budget Constraints
8		Pressure from shareholders	No software to automate graphs
9		Increasing competition based on quality	High cost of implementing Six Sigma
10		Increasing market share through quality	
11			

Gage R&R
(Average and Range Method)

Why?

When?

When you suspect measurement error is contributing to waste, rework, and scrap.

How?

1. Pick 2-3 appraisers

2. Each appraiser measures 10 parts in 2-5 "trials."

3. Put your data into the GageR&R template.

4. Evaluate the results: %R&R measures the appraiser's and gage's contribution to variation. If %R&R<10%, then the measurement system is OK. 10-29% may be OK. 30% needs fixing.

Measurement error can be one of the root causes of waste and rework, especially in manufacturing. Gage Repeatability and Reproducibility (GR&R) helps identify and minimize measurement error.

There are four components of variation 1) the person measuring (Reproducibility: AV-appraiser variation), 2) the gage equipment (Repeatability: EV-equipment variation), 3) interaction of appraiser and gage (R&R), and 4) part variation (PV). Part variation should account for most of the variation, not the appraiser or gage!

Gage R&R (Average &Range		Part 1	2	3	4	5	6	7	8	9	10	Sum	
Appraiser 1	Trial 1	0.65	1	0.85	0.85	0.55	1	0.95	0.85	1	0.6	16.550	0.83
	Trial2	0.6	1	0.8	0.95	0.45	1	0.95	0.8	1	0.7		0.825
	Trial3												
	Trial4										Xbar1		Reference
	Trial 5										0.8275		0.808
	Total	1.25	2	1.65	1.8	1	2	1.9	1.65	2	1.3		Bias
	Average	0.625	1	0.825	0.9	0.5	1	0.95	0.825	1	0.65	Rbar1	0.020
	Range1	0.05	0	0.05	0.1	0.1	0	0	0.05	0	0.1		0.045
Appraiser 2	Trial 1	0.55	1.05	0.8	0.8	0.4	1	0.95	0.75	1	0.55	15.350	
	Trial2	0.55	0.95	0.75	0.75	0.4	1.05	0.9	0.7	0.95	0.5		
	Trial3												
	Trial4										Xbar2		Reference
	Trial 5										0.7675		0.808
	Total	1.1	2	1.55	1.55	0.8	2.05	1.85	1.45	1.95	1.05		Bias
	Average	0.55	1	0.775	0.775	0.4	1.025	0.925	0.725	0.975	0.525	Rbar2	-0.040
	Range2	0	0.1	0.05	0.05	0	0.05	0.05	0.05	0.05	0.05		0.045
Appraiser 3	Trial 1	0.5	1.05	0.8	0.8	0.45	1	0.95	0.8	1.05	0.85	16.550	
	Trial 2	0.55	1	0.8	0.8	0.5	1.05	0.95	0.8	1.05	0.8		
	Trial3												
	Trial4										Xbar3		Reference
	Trial 5										0.8275		0.808
	Total	1.05	2.05	1.6	1.6	0.95	2.05	1.9	1.6	2.1	1.65		Bias
	Average	0.525	1.025	0.8	0.8	0.475	1.025	0.95	0.8	1.05	0.825	Rbar3	0.020
	Range3	0.05	0.05	0	0	0.05	0	0	0	0	0.05		0.025
	K3		3.65	2.7	2.3	2.08	1.93	1.82	1.74	1.67	1.62		
Part	Average	0.567	1.008	0.800	0.825	0.458	1.017	0.942	0.783	1.008	0.667	0.558	Range Avg
	Sum	3.400	6.050	4.800	4.950	2.750	6.100	5.650	4.700	6.050	4.000	48.450	Total

		Constants						
Range Average	0.0383							
XDiff	0.0600	5 Trials	4 Trials	3 Trials	2 Trials	# Trials	2	
UCL	0.1254		2.11	2.28	2.58	3.27	D4	3.27	UCL represents the limit of the individual R's
LCL	0.0000		0	0	0	0	D3	0	Circle those beyond the limit.
Repeatability(EV)	0.1748		2.21	2.5	3.05	4.56	K1	4.56	Identify and correct cause
Reproducibility(AV)	0.1572		3.65	2.7			K2	2.7	LCL = 0 D3=0 for up to 7 trials
Gage Capability(R&R)	0.2351	2 Ops	3 Operators					
Spec Tolerance	0.5000							
Acceptability(%)	0.47	Gage system may be acceptable based on importance of application and cost						

AIAG - Automotive	Using TV	% using Spec Tolerance			
EV (Equipment Varia	0.1748			Equipment Variation (EV)	
%EV	18.7%	35.0%	# Parts	#Trials	#Ops	% of Total Variation (TV)
AV: (Appraiser Varia	0.1572		10	2	3	Appraiser Variation (AV)
%AV	16.8%	31.4%				% of Total Variation (TV)
R&R (Gage Capabilit	0.2351				Repeatability and Reproducibility (R&R)
%R&R	25.2%	47.0%				% of Total Variation (TV)
PV (Part Variation)	0.9045				Part Variation (PV)
%PV	96.8%	180.9%				% of Total Variation (TV)
TV (Total Variation)	0.9348				Total Variation (TV)

If repeatability is larger than reproducibility:
1. gage instrument needs maintenance
2. gage needs to be redesigned
3. clamping or location needs to be improved
4. excessive within-part variation

If reproducibility is larger than repeatability:
1. Operator needs to be trained in how to use and read gage
2. Calibrations on gage are not clear
3. Fixture required to help operator use gage consistently.

Range)	1	
Trial 1	0.65	Same
Trial2	0.6	appraiser gets
Trial3	0.65	different
Trial4	0.55	results.
Trial 5	0.6	

Gage R&R (Average &Range)		1	
Appraiser 1	Trial 1	0.65	
	Trial2	0.65	
	Trial3	0.65	
	Trial4	0.6	
	Trial 5	0.65	Different
	Total	3.2	appraisers get
	Average-A	0.64	different
	Range1	0.05	results.
Appraiser 2	Trial 1	0.6	
	Trial2	0.6	
	Trial3	0.6	
	Trial4	0.55	
	Trial 5	0.6	
	Total	2.95	
	Average-A	0.59	
	Range2	0.05	

Gage R&R
(Anova Method)

Why?

Another way to evaluate GageR&R.

When?

When you have access to Excel to handle the analysis.

There are four components of variation 1) the person measuring (Reproducibility: AV-appraiser variation), 2) the gage equipment (Repeatability: EV-equipment variation), 3) interaction of appraiser and part, and 4) part variation (PV). Part variation should account for most of the variation, not the appraiser or gage!

How?

1. Pick 2-3 appraisers

2. Each appraiser measures 10 parts in 2-5 "trials."

3. Using the Anova calculations, evaluate GageR&R.

	A	B	C	D	E	F	G
50	**Calculate GageR&R using Anova**						
51	**Anova Source**	df	SS	MS	F		
52	Appraiser	2	0.0480	0.02400			
53	Parts	9	2.0587	0.22875			
54	Appraiser x Part	18	0.1037	0.00576	4.4588		
55	Gage Error	30	0.0387	0.00129			
56	Total	59	2.24913				
57							
58		Estimate of Variance	Std. Dev		5.15* Stdev	% Study Variation	% Contribution
59	Repeatability	0.00129	0.03594	EV	0.1851	18%	3%
60	Appraiser	0.000912	0.0302	AV	0.1555	15%	2%
61	AppraiserxPart	0.002234	0.04726	INT	0.2434	23%	5%
62	R&R	0.00444	0.06661	R&R	0.3431	33%	11%
63	Part	0.03716	0.19278	PV	0.9928	95%	89%
64				TV	1.0504		

Range Method

How?

1. Two appraisers measure 5 parts.

2. Input tolerance or variation to determine R&R

	A	B	C	D	E	F	G	H
1	**Range Method**							
2	Part	1	2	3	4	5	Average	
3	**Appraiser 1**	0.85	0.75	1	0.45	0.5	0.71	
4	**Appraiser 2**	0.8	0.7	0.95	0.55	0.6	0.72	d2
5	Range	0.05	0.05	0.05	0.1	0.1	0.07	1.19
6								
7	GR&R	0.303						
8	Process Variation (or tolerance)	0.40						
9	%GR&R	75.7%						

Gage R&R
(Bias and Linearity)

Why?

When?

1. Evaluate and accept new or repaired gages
2. Evaluate suspect gages

How?

1. Pick five different parts with accurate reference values (measured by best gauges).

2. Measure each part 12 times with the same gage.

3. Evaluate the gage's ability to stay accurate over a range of values. Lower slope (flatter line) = better gage linearity)

Evaluate the accuracy of a gage and its ability to measure accurately over a range of values.

Bias evaluates the difference between a part's *reference value* (usually measured by highly accurate equipment) and its *measured value* (i.e., accuracy using standard gages).

Linearity evaluates whether measurement bias changes over a range of measured values.

	A	B	C	D	E	F
1		Part				
2	Trials	1	2	3	4	5
3	1	2.7	5.1	5.8	7.6	9.1
4	2	2.5	3.9	5.7	7.7	9.3
5	3	2.4	4.2	5.9	7.8	9.5
6	4	2.5	5.0	5.9	7.7	9.3
7	5	2.7	3.8	6.0	7.8	9.4
8	6	2.3	3.9	6.1	7.8	9.5
9	7	2.5	3.9	6.0	7.8	9.5
10	8	2.5	3.9	6.1	7.7	9.5
11	9	2.4	3.9	6.4	7.8	9.6
12	10	2.4	4.0	6.3	7.5	9.2
13	11	2.6	4.1	6.0	7.6	9.3
14	12	2.4	3.8	6.1	7.7	9.4
15	Average	2.49	4.13	6.03	7.71	9.38
16	Reference Value	2.00	4.00	6.00	8.00	10.00
17	Bias	0.49	0.12	0.02	-0.29	-0.62
18	Range	0.40	1.30	0.70	0.30	0.50
19	bias= slope*ref+b	0.473333	0.21	-0.05333	-0.31667	-0.58
20	Slope=	-0.13167				
21	Y intercept b=	0.736667				
22	Goodness of fit	0.977907				
23	Process Variation	2.488105				
24	Linearity	0.3276				
25	%Linearity	13%				

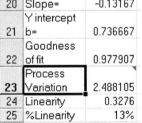

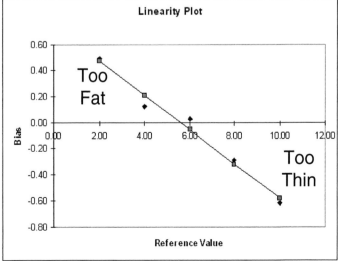

Linearity Plot

Ishikawa Diagram
(Cause-Effect)

Why?

When?

To analyze the root causes of a problem.

Identify the root causes of defects. Like weeds, all problems have various root causes. Remove the roots and, like magic, the weeds disappear.

How?

1. Put the problem statement in the head of the fish and the major causes at the end of the bones:
   * Processes, machines, materials, measurement, people, environment
   * Steps of a process
2. For each cause, ask "Why?" up to five times.
3. Circle one-to-five <u>root</u> causes (end of "why" chain)
4. Verify the root causes with data (Pareto, Scatter, etc.)

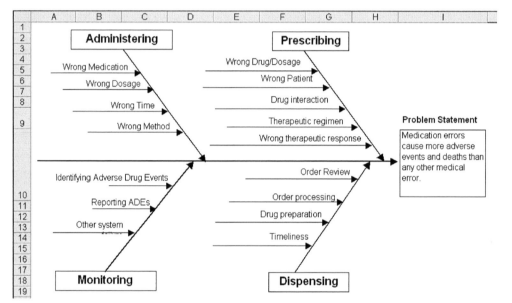

Matrix

Why?

When?

To prioritize or focus decision making, and to identify relationships among variables.

How?

1. **Generate two or more sets of characteristics** to be compared. Use tree diagrams or brainstorming.

2. **Choose the proper matrix** to represent the interactions (L, T, X, Y).

3. **Put the characteristics on the axes** of the matrix.

4. **Rank the interactions** from 1 (low) to 5 (high).

The matrix diagram helps prioritize tasks or issues in ways that aid decision making; identify the connecting points between large groups of characteristics, functions, and tasks; or show the ranking or priority of an interaction.

Matrices can be used in many ways to show relationships. They can be shaped like an L (see countermeasures matrix), a T, an X, or a three-dimensional, inverted Y.

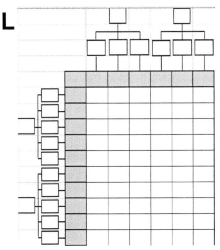

L

T

X

	A	B	C	D	E	F	G	H
1	Problem Statement:	From October to November, server availability averaged 100,000 minutes of downtime per week.						
2	Root Cause	Countermeasure	Feasibility	Specific Actions	Effectiveness	Overall	Action (Who?)	Value ($/week)
3	Corrupted Password files	Upgrade to latest operating system	4	Develop and implement installation plan across server environment.	5	20	MI S	$14,667
4	Application Design problems	Maintenance release of applications	4	Identify changes in design and implement changes	4	16	IT	$3,667
5						0		
6				Feasibility: 1-low, 5-high		Effectiveness: 1-low, 5-high		
7				1-Expensive & Difficult to implement		1-Not very effective		
8				5-Inexpensive and easy to implement		5-Very Effective		
9								

Measures Matrix

Why?

When?

When beginning to monitor any process.

How?

1. **Identify the customer's requirements** in their language.

2. **Choose the proper measurement** that will monitor that requirement.

3. **Identify how often it will be measured (period).**

Define specific ways to measure the customer's requirements and to predict the stability and capability of the process.

| Requirement | Indicators | | Period |
	Quality or Process		
Better	Number of defects Percent defective (number of defects/total)		minute hour day
Faster	# or % of commitments missed time in minutes, hours, days		week month
Cheaper	cost per unit cost of waste or rework		shift batch

	A	B	C	D
1		**Measurements**		
2		Customer:	Product/Service:	
3		**Customer Requirements**	**Measurement**	**Period**
4	**Better**	Treat me like you want my business	Customer Complaints	
5		Deliver products that meet my needs		
6		Products/services that work right	% defective	
7		Be accurate, right the first time		
8				
9		Fix it right the first time	Number/% repeat repairs	
10				
11	**Faster**	I want it when I want it	Cycle time	per product
12		Make commitments that meet my needs	% first choice commitment	
13		Meet you commitments	% commitments missed	Daily
14		I want fast, easy access to help	% calls answered < 60 sec and %calls referred	Daily
15		Don't waste my time		
16				
17		if it breaks, fix it fast	Repair cycle time	per repair
18				
19	**Cheaper**	Deliver irresistable value		
20		Help me save money		
21		Help me save time		
22				
23				
24				

QI Macros Example Book

PDPC Chart
(Tree Diagram)

Why?   Anticipate problems before implementation.

When?

To evaluate new, unique or complex implementation plans when cost of failure may be high.

How?

1. Identify the high level steps and sequence of the plan.

2. Identify what could go wrong.

3. Identify possible counter-measures for each potential problem.

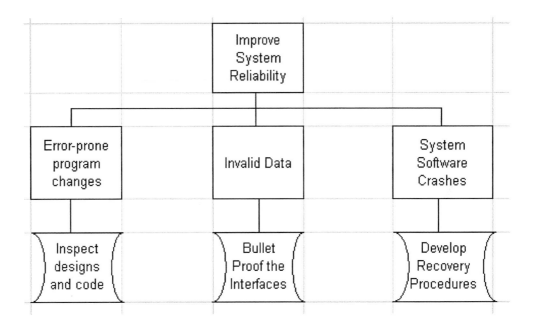

PreControl Chart

Why?

When?

To evaluate new, unique or complex implementation plans when cost of failure may be high.

How?

1. Enter the upper and lower specification limits into the data sheet.

2. Add data as you begin to run the process.

3. Evaluate the process much like you would a control chart. Most points should land in the green or yellow. Too many in the red: Danger! May miss customer specifications.

To evaluate a process before you have enough data (20 samples) to do a control chart or histogram.

	A	B	C	D	E	F	G
1	LSL=	10			USL=	30	
2	X Axis	Red	Yellow	Green	Yellow	Red	Data
3	1	10	5	10	5	10	15
4	2	10	5	10	5	10	20
5	3	10	5	10	5	10	17
6	4	10	5	10	5	10	
7	5	10	5	10	5	10	
8	6	10	5	10	5	10	

Pre Control Chart

Pugh Concept Selection Matrix
(Design for Six Sigma)

Why?

When?

To evaluate various design alternatives against an existing baseline.

In QFD or evaluating countermeasures.

How?

1. Identify the criteria or requirements.

2. Identify the various design alternatives.

3. Rate each concept against each criteria as better than, worse than, or the same as the baseline.

4. Select the optimum design alternative (more +'s).

	A	B	C	D	E	F	G	H	I
					Design Concepts				
1	**Pugh Concept Selection Matrix Comparison Criteria**	Current Process (Baseline)	Plug and Play	Bolt and Screw		Concept 4	Concept 5	Concept 6	Concept 7
2	Faster Assembly		+	-					
3	Harder to accidentally disconnect		-	S					
4									
5	Criteria								
6	Criteria								
7									
8									
9									
10	Total +'s		1	0	0	0	0	0	0
11	Total -'s		1	1	0	0	0	0	0
12									
13	Compare current with		+ Better Alternative						
14	selected alternatives		- Worse Alternative						
15			S Same Alternative						
16									
17			Focus on alternative with the most +'s and fewest -'s						

QFD House of Quality
(Design for Six Sigma)

Why?

When?

Designing new products and processes to achieve Six Sigma.

How?

1.**Service**: Gather the Voice of the Customer through surveys and analysis of customer correspondence and complaints. Develop and analyze the design requirements (House of Quality).

2. **Delivery**: Develop a "blueprint" of the delivery process.

3. **Materials** Identify the people, process, and technology needed to establish and maintain product and service delivery.

4. **Operations**: Act to implement process.

QFD (Quality Function Deployment) is a rigorous planning process to ensure that customer's requirements will be satisfied. It can slash the time required to design new products or services, and it can be used to reengineer business processes.

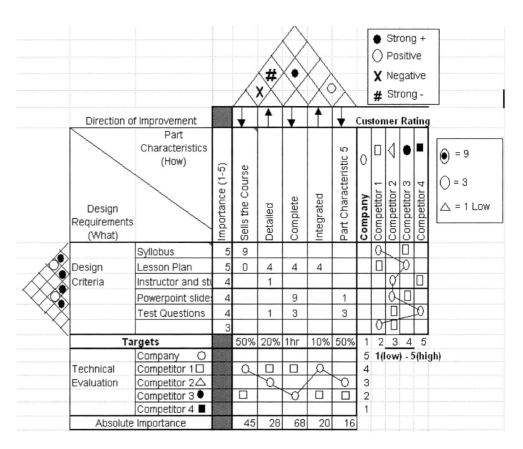

QI Macros Example Book

Relationship/Systems Diagrams

Why?

When?

After problem solving to identify plan for implementing changes.

How?

1. **State the system, problem or issue** under discussion

2. **Draw one-way arrows to indicate the cause-effect relationship** among the components of the diagram.

3. **Identify the effects.** If an *increase* in A causes an increase in B, put an "S" (same) on the arrow. If an *increase* in A causes a *decrease* in B, put an "O" (opposite) on the arrow.

The systems diagram shows the cause-effect relationships among many key elements. It can be used to identify the causes of problems or to work backward from a desired outcome to identify all of the causal factors that would need to exist to ensure the achievement of an outcome.

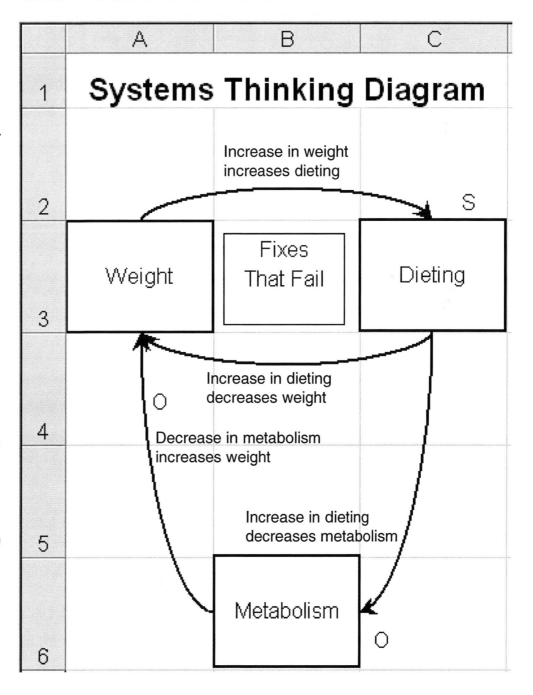

Sample Size Calculator

Why?

When?

To estimate the number of samples required for a certain level of confidence.

How?

1. Select a desired confidence level (80, 90, 95,99%)

Attribute Data

2. If the percent defects is known, enter it, otherwise assume 50%.

Variable data:

2. Set the confidence interval.

3. If the standard deviation is known, enter it. Otherwise estimate as 1/6th of the range.

The sample size calculator will help you determine the number of samples needed to achieve a desired level of confidence in your results.

	A	B
1	Confidence Level	95%
2	Confidence Interval	2
3	Population (if known)	
4		
5	**Attribute Data**	
6	Percent defects (50%)	50%
7	Sample Size (Unknown Population)	0
8	Sample Size for Known Population	
9		
10	**Variable Data**	
11	Standard Deviation ([High-Low]/6)	10
12	Sample Size (Unknown Population)	96
13	Sample Size for Known Population	

Example 1 - Sampling to determine battery life

- Estimate must be within 2 hours (confidence interval) of true mean
- Standard Deviation = 10.0 hours
- 95% confidence level

n= 96

	A	B
1	Confidence Level	95%
2	Confidence Interval	0.001
3	Population (if known)	
4		
5	**Attribute Data**	
6	Percent defects (50%)	50%
7	Sample Size (Unknown Population)	960400
8	Sample Size for Known Population	
9		
10	**Variable Data**	
11	Standard Deviation ([High-Low]/6)	0.003
12	Sample Size (Unknown Population)	35
13	Sample Size for Known Population	

Example 2 - Determine Average Part Length

- Most production between 2.009 (low) and 2.027 (high) inches
- Estimate Stdev as (2.027-2.009)/6 = .003 inches
- Confidence interval = +/- 0.001

n=35

Targets and Means Matrix

Why?

When?
To deploy quality planning objectives.

How?

1. **Identify the targets.**

2. **Identify the means** to achieve the targets.

3. **Rank the ability of the means to achieve the targets.**

4. **Identify the resources required.**

5. **Identify who** is responsible for achieving the target.

6. **Establish an implementation timeline.**

Project manage the means to achieve quality targets.

	A	B	C	D	E	F	G	H	I	J	K
1								Targets and Means Matrix			
2				Objectives				Action Plan			
3		⊙ = 9 High ○ = 3 △ = 1 Low	Target 1 (Reduce/Increase)	Target 2	Target 3	Target 4	Target 5	Resources Required	Who?	Measure	Time J F M A M J J A S O N D
4	Speed		1								
5	Quality		9	3		1					
6	Value			1							
7	Cycle time				9		1				
8	Defects				1	3	3				
9	Cost										
10			50%	20%	1hr	10%	50%				
11				Targets							

(Column A rows 4–9 labeled **Means**)

Time Tracking Template

Why?

When?

To accelerate any process, you have to be able to measure and improve the key steps in that process.

How?

1. Click on the cells in columns A, C and D to populate the current date and time. C is the process start time and D is the stop time.

2. Populate columns B, E and F with other information about each event.

3. Column G is calculated as the difference between the start and stop time. H converts G to minutes.

4. Select the data in column H to run a chart.

To automate the collection of data for the time between steps within a process (minutes, hours, days, etc).

	A	B	C	D	E	F	G	H
			Start	Times			Total Time Start to End hh:mm	Total Time Start to End Minutes
1	Date	Ref #:	Step 1	End Time	Who?	Reason for Delay		
2	05/18/07	409	09:33	09:53	JS	No Equipment	0:20	20
3	05/19/07	123	11:30	12:05	LJ	Miscommunication	0:35	35
4	05/23/07	546	07:08	07:49	LJ	No Staff	0:40	40
5	06/20/07	789	11:53	12:23	JA		0:30	30
6	06/20/07	125	12:40	12:59	AA		0:19	19
7								

To edit dates or times in columns A, C and D, click on the cell you want to edit and make changes in Excel's formula bar window.

▼		*fx* 6/20/2007 12:59:14 PM	
B	C	D	E

Transition Planning Matrix

Establish a plan to move the company from one level of performance to another (e.g., 3 sigma to 5 sigma).

Why?

When?

When the change involves the whole organization or department.

How?

1. **Pick one of the three strategies to maximize.** Optimize the other two in service of the main one.

2. **Describe the "current state"** of your process, organization, and technology.

3. **Imagine the future state** where you are "world class."

4. **Design and align the interim steps** to become world class.

Process Title

Dimension / Strategy	Current Environment (Maximize Customer Satisfaction, Operational Efficiency or Innovation)	Simplify and Stabilize (Increasing complexity often requires initial simplification and stabilization)	Maximize or Optimize (Then maximize or optimize your strategy, process, organization, and technology)	Expand Into New Domains (Successful business evolution invites application in new arenas)	Competitive Advantage (Which brings competitive advantage)	Becoming World Class (Which leads to world leadership in your chosen discipline)
Customer/Employee Satisfaction						
Operational Effectiveness (speed, quality, and low cost)						
Innovation						
Processes						
Understand Your Customer						
Involve Customers in Design						
Marketing and Selling						
Involve Customers in Delivery						
Customer Service						
Manage Client Information						
Organization						
Organizational Structure						
Organizational Role						
Accountability and Rewards						
Core Competencies						
Employee Development						
Technology						
Architecture						
Data						
Business Rules						
Software/Hardware Environment						
Network						

Tree Diagram

Why?

When?

Develop a "Master Improvement Story" or Balanced Scorecard.

How?

1. Start with a high level objective (e.g., reduce defects or delay).

2. Layout long-term and short-term strategies and tactics for achieving the objective.

3. Identify objective measures and targets for each measure.

Systematically lay out goals and linkages from the highest level to the lowest.

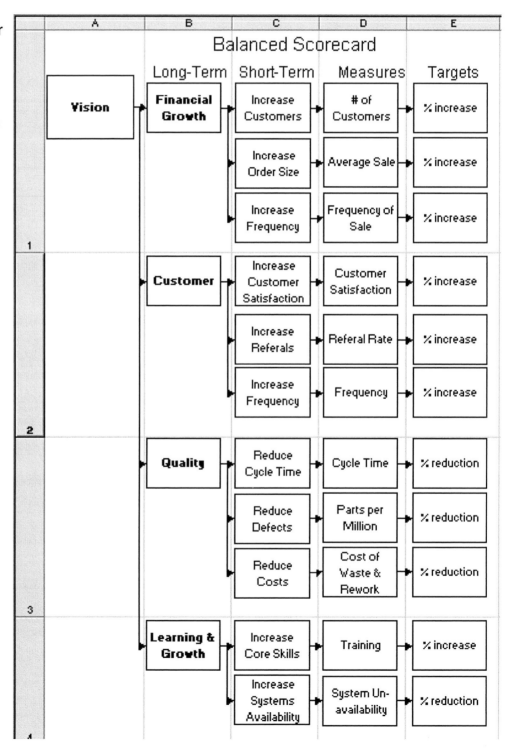

Value Added Matrix

Why?

When?

To slash cycle time and double your speed.

How?

1. For each arrow, box, and diamond, list its function and the time spent.

2. Now become the customer's order and ask:
   - Is the order delayed?
   - Is this inspection necessary?
   - Does it "add value," or is this just waste or rework?

3. Most of the delay is in the arrows. How can delays be eliminated or shortened to accelerate your productivity?

Identify the waste, rework, and delay that can be eliminated from the process.

	A	B	C	D	E
1		**Value Added Checklist**			
2	**Activity, Decision, Arrow**	Time Spent (hours, days, weeks, months)	Adds Value (not inspection or fix-it work)	Changes Product or Service Physically	Right The First Time (not waste or rework)
3	Claim Received	1 min	Y	Y	Y
4	Arrow to Establish Control	5 day	N	N	N
5	Establish Control	-	Y	Y	Y
6	Arrow to Create Folder	10 min	N	N	N
7	Create Folder	-	Y	Y	Y
8	Arrow to Need Evidence?	25 days	N	N	N
9	Need Evidence? (inspection/decision)	3 min	N	N	Y
10	No: Arrow to Exam Needed?	2 days	N	N	N
11	Yes: Arrow To Request Evidence	1 day	N	N	N
12	Request Evidence	45 min	Y	Y	Y
13	Arrow to Evidence Received? 90	60 days	N	N	N
14	Evidence Received? Days	-	N	N	Y
15	No: Arrow to Provide Letter	5-10 days	N	N	N
16	Yes: Arrow to Exam Needed?	2 days	N	N	N
17	Provide Letter	30 min	Y	Y	Y
18	Arrow to Exam Needed?	30 days	N	N	N
19	Exam Needed? (decision)	15 min	Y	Y	Y
20	No: Arrow to Rate Claim	-	N	N	N
21	Yes: Arrow to Request Exam	-	N	N	N
22	Request Exam	1 hour	Y	Y	Y
23	Arrow to Exam Complete? 36	-	N	N	N
24	Exam Complete? (decision) Days	25 days	N	N	Y
25	No: Arrow to Request Exam	-	N	N	N
26	Yes: Arrow to Rate Claim	90-100 days	N	N	N
27	Rate Claim	3 hours	Y	Y	Y
28	Arrow to Claims Review	1 day	N	N	N
29	Claims Review	2 days	N	N	Y
30	Arrow to Error Noted?	-	N	N	N
31	Error Noted? (Inspection/decision)	-	N	N	N
32	No: Arrow to Prepare Award	3-14 days	N	N	N
33	Yes: Arrow to Rate Claim (rework) 120	1 day	N	N	N
34	Prepare Award Days	15 min	Y	Y	Y
35	Arrow to Rating Correction Needed?	-	N	N	N
36	Rating Correction Needed? (Decision)	-	N	N	Y
37	No: Arrow to Authorizer Review	2 days	N	N	N
38	Yes: Arrow to Rate Claim (rework)	-	N	N	N
39	Authorizer Review	8 min	N	N	Y
40	Arrow to Rating Correction Needed?	-	N	N	N
41	No: Arrow To Award Correction Needed?	-	N	N	N
42	Yes: Arrow to Rate Claim (rework)	-	N	N	N
43	Award Correction Needed?	-	N	N	Y
44	No: Arrow to Authorize Award	-	N	N	N
45	Yes: Arrow to Prepare Award (Rework)	-	N	N	N
46	Authorize Award	-	Y	Y	Y
47	Arrow to Mail Award Notice	-	Y	Y	Y

Value Stream Map

Define the <u>existing</u> or improved value stream as a starting point for removing non-value added delay and activities.

Why?

When?

To analyze Value-Added and non-value added activities and delays.

How?

1. Start with high level process steps.

2. Identify delays between steps and inventory levels.

3. Use Post-it™ notes to lay out activities, arrows and work in process.

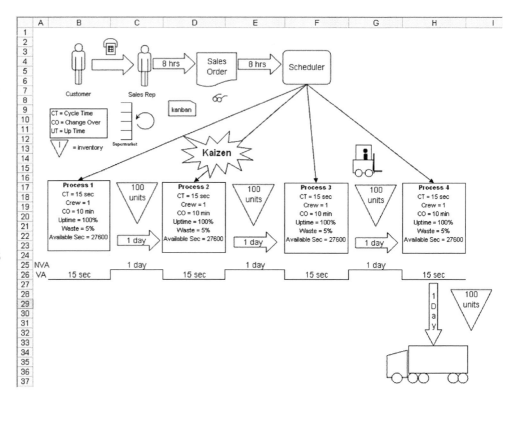

Voice of the Customer

Gather the customer's needs and wants as a basis for establishing objectives.

Why?

When?

Before creating a Balanced Scorecard or selecting measurements.

How?

1 Enter key customer statements on left. Rate the importance from 1 (low) to 5 (high).

2 Identify and enter key business functions along the top.

3. For each center box, rate the "how" (top) to the "what" (left). Multiply times the importance to get the total weight.

4. Highest scores show where to focus your improvement efforts.

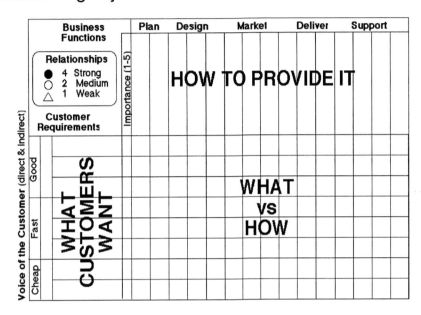

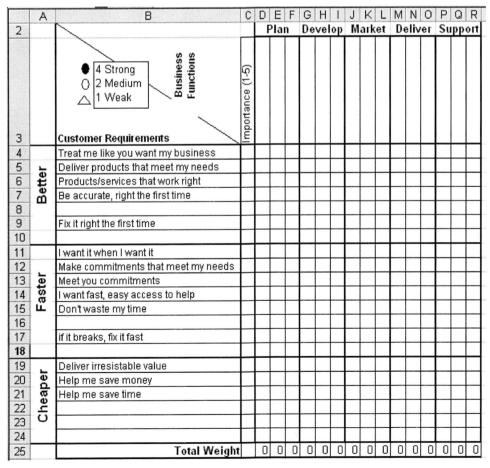

Laser Focus the Improvement

Your "Million Dollar Money Belt" Improvement Strategy

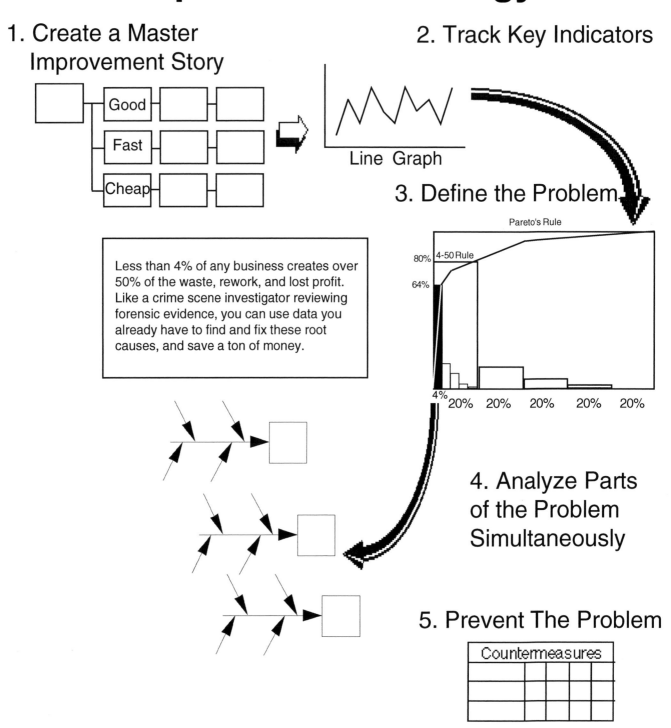

1. Create a Master Improvement Story

Good

Fast

Cheap

2. Track Key Indicators

Line Graph

3. Define the Problem

Pareto's Rule

4-50 Rule

80%

64%

4%

20% 20% 20% 20% 20%

Less than 4% of any business creates over 50% of the waste, rework, and lost profit. Like a crime scene investigator reviewing forensic evidence, you can use data you already have to find and fix these root causes, and save a ton of money.

4. Analyze Parts of the Problem Simultaneously

5. Prevent The Problem

Countermeasures

Sustain the Improvement

Monitor and Sustain
New Levels of Performance in
Mission Critical Systems

1. Refine the Process

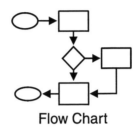

Flow Chart

2. Analyze Stability

Control Charts
(Stability)

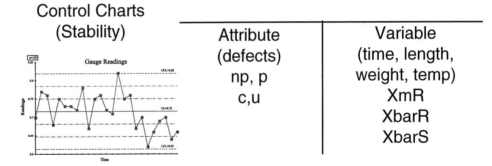

Attribute (defects) np, p c,u	Variable (time, length, weight, temp) XmR XbarR XbarS

3. Analyze Capability

Histogram
(Capability)

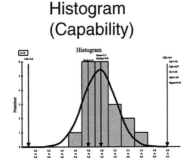

Design for Reliability

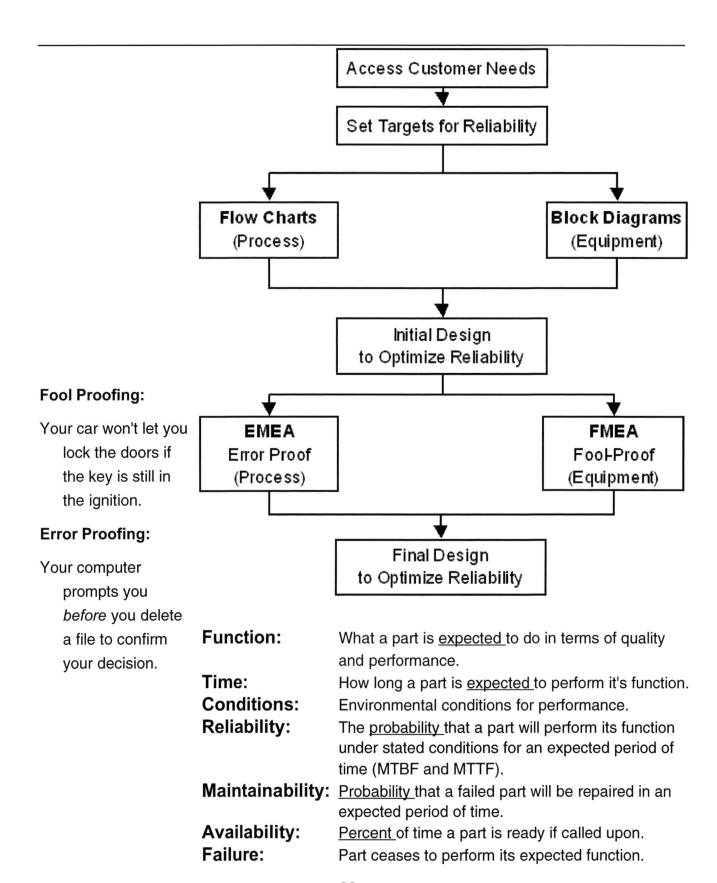

Fool Proofing:

Your car won't let you lock the doors if the key is still in the ignition.

Error Proofing:

Your computer prompts you *before* you delete a file to confirm your decision.

Function:	What a part is <u>expected</u> to do in terms of quality and performance.
Time:	How long a part is <u>expected</u> to perform it's function.
Conditions:	Environmental conditions for performance.
Reliability:	The <u>probability</u> that a part will perform its function under stated conditions for an expected period of time (MTBF and MTTF).
Maintainability:	<u>Probability</u> that a failed part will be repaired in an expected period of time.
Availability:	<u>Percent</u> of time a part is ready if called upon.
Failure:	Part ceases to perform its expected function.

QI Macros Example Book

QI Macros and Data Mining
One-Day Workshop

Learning Objectives:
- Use the QI Macros to automate all of the graphs and documents needed for Process Improvement and Stabilization.
- Select charts based on the type of data.
- Use the advanced control chart features.
- Use Excel's PivotTable function to find the improvement project lurking in your data.

Workshop Outline:

Creating and Analyzing Charts with the QI Macros
- Pareto Charts
- Scatter Diagrams
- Control Charts and Stability Analysis
  - Types of Data – Choosing the Right Chart
  - Analyzing Stability
  - Show Process Change and Other advanced chart functions
- Histograms and Capability Analysis (Cp, Cpk)
- Demonstration and practice with participants own data

Fill in the Blank Templates
- Chart Templates
- Templates using Excels Drawing Tools

Anova and Analysis Tools

Data Transformation Tools
- Stack/Restack
- Word Count

Data Mining with PivotTables
- Cross Tab PivotTable Wizard
- Demonstration and practice with participants own data

Course Materials for Each Participant
- QI Macros SPC Software for Excel - full version or 30 day evaluation copy
- SPC Quick Reference Card
- QI Macros Training CD (optional 49.95 each)

Course Length: 8 hours   **Participants:** up to 25

Investment Options (pricing good thru 12/31/2010):

1. $8,500 including U.S. travel, and all training materials and QI Macros software for all 25 participants.

2. $6,000 with 30-day evaluation version of the QI Macros SPC Software.

3. $14,500 - Option 1 plus an additional day of individual and/or team coaching/ to analyze data or develop improvement projects. (Must be the day before or after training.)

Qty.	Item	Order Form	Price	FedEx	Mail	Total
	230	QI Macros for Excel (discounts for 2 or more)	$199	$25	$8	
	237	QI Macros Training CD	$ 49.95	$25	$6	
	208	Lean Simplified Book	$ 9.95	$25	$6	
	205	Six Sigma Simplified Green Belt Training Workbook	$ 29.95	$25	$6	
	210	Six Sigma Instructor Guide–Green Belt Training Made Easy	$ 39.95	$25	$6	
	225	Lean Six Sigma Simplified (5 CDs)	$ 97	$25	$10	
	265	Six Sigma Green Belt Training Video on 2 DVDs + Guide	$197	$25	$10	
	215	SPC Simplified Book	$29.95	$25	$6	
	267	SPC Simplified Video on DVD + Guide (☐ Mfg ☐ Healthcare)	$ 97	$25	$10	
	262	Lean Simplified Video on DVD + Lean Simplified #208	$ 97	$25	$10	
	263	Lean for Healthcare Labs on 2 DVDs + Lean Simplified #208	$197	$25	$10	
Shipping and Handling		**First individual item**				
U.S.		**Each additional Item: $2 (Mail) or $5 (FedEx)**				
					Order Total	

Please type or print clearly or attach business card here

Company _____

Your Name _____

Mailing Address _____

P.O. Box _____ Apt/Ste. _____

City, ST, Zip _____

Phone _____

Fax _____

Email _____
☐ Check here if you have ordered from us before

Yes! We also accept Purchase Orders!

Purchase Order Number _____
(to prevent duplicate shipments, <u>never</u> send confirming POs)

☐ VISA ☐ MasterCard ☐ AMEX
_____ Exp._____
Signature _____

☐ I've enclosed my check, VISA, MasterCard, or AmEx.
☐ I want to try them out **Absolutely Risk Free**. Please send my order immediately. *I have 30 days to pay the invoice or return them with no obligation.*

Order by 12/31/2010 to Receive these Special Bonuses:

Special Bonus #1 - Lean Quick Reference Card
Special Bonus #2 - Six Sigma Quick Reference Card
Special Bonus #3 - SPC Quick Reference Card

Orders Only
(To minimize errors please order on-line)

Order On-line at: www.qimacros.com

FAX your order to: (888) 468-1536 Toll Free or
(303) 753-9675

Mail to: KnowWare International Inc
2253 S. Oneida St. Ste. 3D Denver, CO 80224

Orders-only, Call Toll-free: (888) 468-1535 or
(Please have your item # ready) (303) 757-2039

Questions about the QI Macros?
email: info@qimacros.com 9 a.m. to 5 p.m. MST
(888) 468-1537 Toll Free or (303) 756-9144

90 Day, Unconditional, No Risk, Money-back Guarantee